FORENSIC SOCIAL WORK:
LEGAL ASPECTS
OF PROFESSIONAL PRACTICE
Robert L. Barker, DSW
Douglas M. Branson, JD

SOME ADVANCE REVIEWS

"Provides explicit, practical information on a variety of current and emerging legal issues that practicing social workers must know. . . . Of particular interest is the authors' consideration of the conflict between the therapist's duty to maintain confidentiality and the duty to disclose to others or warn the potential victim of possible harm from a client. Barker and Branson's unique work is a valuable, welcome, and highly useful contribution to social work literature."

Sol Gothard, JD, MSW, ACSW, Judge, Fifth Circuit Court of Appeal, State of Louisiana; Full Professor, Graduate School of Social Work, Tulane University

"Provides a useful primer on this critically important subject. . . . A comprehensive overview of a wide range of pertinent topics, including courtroom tactics, the intersection of laws and ethics, the use of contracts, civil litigation, the legal regulation of social work, peer adjudication, and recording. The authors' practical advice and tips concerning courtroom strategy and behavior are especially useful."

Frederic G. Reamer, PhD, Professor, School of Social Work, Rhode Island College

Forensic Social Work
Legal Aspects of Professional Practice

HAWORTH Social Work Practice
Carlton E. Munson, DSW, Senior Editor

Forensic Social Work
Legal Aspects
of Professional Practice

Robert L. Barker, DSW
Douglas M. Branson, JD

The Haworth Press
New York • London • Norwood (Australia)

The Haworth Press, Inc., 10 Alice Street, Binghamton, NY 13904-1580

Library of Congress Cataloging-in-Publication Data

Barker, Robert L.
    Forensic social work : legal aspects of professional practice / Robert L. Barker, Douglas M. Branson.
       p. cm.
    Includes bibliographical references and index.
    ISBN 1-56024-351-1 (alk. paper).
    1. Social workers—Legal status, laws, etc.—United States. I. Branson, Douglas M. II. Title.
KF3721.B37   1992
344.73'0313—dc20
[347.304313]
                                                     92-31570
                                                        CIP

CONTENTS

ABOUT THE AUTHORS

Robert L. Barker, DSW, is Professor of Social Work at the Catholic University of America in Washington, DC. He has worked as a social worker in juvenile courts and as an expert witness in numerous family custody legal disputes. The author of sixteen books, Dr. Barker is a member of the National Association of Social Workers, the American Association for Marital and Family Therapy, and the National Academy of Practice in Social Work.

Douglas M. Branson, JD, is Professor of Law at the University of Puget Sound in Tacoma, Washington. He is the author of three books and over eighty articles on legal aspects of professional and corporate practices. A legal consultant to various social activist organizations and professional societies, Dr. Branson is a member of the American Bar Association, the Washington Bar Association, and the American Law Institute.

Preface and Acknowledgments

Social workers have growing interest in the legal aspects of their professional practice. This interest is stimulated by the increased litigiousness of modern society, the growing demand for social work expertise in legal settings, and the trend toward legal regulation of professions. As a result, social workers require as much information as possible about these trends and their own role therein. This book seeks to help meet that need.

Because Forensic Social Work is a specialty that exists at the interface between the social work profession and the legal profession, any serious work about it must draw heavily on the knowledge from both disciplines. Accordingly, the authors of this book, a social worker and a lawyer, have drawn on the knowledge of their respective colleagues.

Many social workers and lawyers have been called upon for information, examples, resources, and advice in the production of this book. They include Jackson Rose, William Oltman, Lloyd Johnson, John Michael Seelig, John and Sally Watkins, Judge Thomas Larkin, and Judge Sol Gothard.

Others have also been most helpful. Bill Cohen and Karen Lee at The Haworth Press have been very encouraging and supportive as they provided considerable competence and focus to this project. So too have our wives, Mary Elizabeth Donovan Barker and Cynthia Branson.

Robert L. Barker
Douglas M. Branson

Chapter 1

Forensic Social Work
in a Litigious Society

Forensic social work is a new professional specialty that focuses on the interface between society's legal and human service systems. It includes such activities as providing expert testimony in courts of law, investigating cases of possible criminal conduct, and assisting the legal system to help resolve such disputes as child custody, divorce, delinquency, nonsupport, mental hospital commitment, and relative's responsibility.

Forensic social work seeks to educate law professionals about people's human service needs; it also educates social work colleagues about the legal aspects of their work. The specialty is oriented to helping social workers avoid becoming defendants in malpractice suits, or when that is unavoidable, to help one side or the other achieve the best possible outcome. Furthermore, forensic social work is interested in the legal regulation of professional practice, including professional licensing and provisions for public accountability.

Such activities are of growing interest and importance for social work. The well-known trend toward litigiousness in modern society is only one of the reasons why. Another is that the laws regarding professional practice have changed dramatically in recent years, especially regarding confidentiality and the legal requirements to control one's clients. And another reason is that virtually every jurisdiction now legally regulates social work practice through licensing laws. Forensic social work is the specialty that has newly emerged within the profession to systematically address these concerns.

1

THE FOUNDATIONS OF FORENSIC SOCIAL WORK

While forensic social work itself is a newly identified specialty, some of its activities are as old as the profession itself. Social work emerged at the beginning of the twentieth century largely to fulfill many legal functions. The earliest social workers investigated families to determine if parents were abusing their children or otherwise not meeting their children's developmental needs. They served as witnesses in law courts, reporting the findings of their social investigations. They worked in prisons and courts as probation officers and in crime-ridden neighborhoods with youth gangs.

Many of the earliest social workers were oriented to changing society and its social injustices. They led political movements to change laws and to get the legal system to enforce existing laws with more rigor. They led successful campaigns to change or enact child labor laws, obtain legal rights for women, and to improve laws that would better protect workers and consumers.

Many of the people who created the social work profession and its employing organizations were lawyers. For example, lawyer Robert Weeks deForest (1866-1948) was a founder and the principal leader of the Charity Organization Societies, the early social agencies where social workers were first employed and given their present name. He also founded the first school for social workers (now known as Columbia University School of Social Work). Florence Kelley (1859-1932), who virtually founded the National Consumer's League and the United States Children's Bureau and who is usually identified as a founder of the social work profession, was also a lawyer. So too was Sophonisba Breckinridge (1866-1948), who brought social work education into the university system and led the movement to include legal courses in the social work education curriculum.

EARLY AFFINITY BETWEEN SOCIAL WORK
AND THE LAW

With such a foundation it was natural for social work to have close ties to the law and legal justice system. Almost every new professional school included many law courses. Field placements were in family courts, prisons, legal aid offices, and even private law firms. Upon graduation, many social workers became probation and parole officers and court investigators. Those who worked in welfare offices, settlement houses, and charity organization societies encountered the victims of crime and injustice and reported their findings to law authorities.

During its first 30 years social work was closer to the law than it is now to the health and mental health fields. Most early social workers belonged to the National Conference on Charities and Corrections (founded in 1879) and a substantial part of its membership was also law officials. The nation's juvenile court system avoided the adversarial procedures of other courts by employing social workers to advocate for the child, family, and state simultaneously. Then the worker would act as probation officer for the judges' sentences of juvenile cases (Stehno, 1987).

The major employers of social workers were public welfare offices and child welfare organizations, and much of their work involved investigating and reporting to the legal authorities the conditions to which children and the disadvantaged were subjected. Many social workers found themselves testifying in courts almost as frequently as they were working with clients. Recognizing that this was becoming a major social work function, the schools of social work increased their offerings of courses in legal aspects of professional practice and encouraged more students to study such offerings.

THE DIVERGENCE BETWEEN LAW AND SOCIAL WORK

It was not until the mid-1930s that social work began its turn away from a legal orientation toward its emphasis on mental health and humanistic concerns. The poverty and economic problems seen in the Great Depression (1929-1941) drew the interests of many social workers away from the law and more toward economics and sociology. The new philosophies of Sigmund Freud (1856-1939) and other psychoanalytic theorists influenced many other social workers toward an interest in the mental processes of individuals.

Many professional schools of social work replaced their course offerings in the legal and justice fields with more courses with psychosocial orientations. Field placements in law settings were replaced by those in mental health clinics. Even though the social work profession recognized and advocated closer relationships with law professionals, few practical steps were made in that direction (Sloan, 1967).

As social workers pursued other interests, prisons, juvenile courts, and the probation system could no longer find enough workers to fill most of their jobs and had to turn to members of other disciplines (Handler, 1976). The National Conference on Charities and Corrections split into two groups reflecting the schism between social workers and the justice/corrections system. With the *In re Gault* decision in 1967, lawyers replaced social workers in the juvenile courts, and by law the youngster's legal rights outweighed all other considerations (Gothard, 1987). In public welfare and child protective service agencies, investigations of potential abuse were increasingly done by individuals who had not been trained as social workers (Kadushin, 1987).

The legal regulation of social work practice was also given little emphasis. Before the 1970s the predominant view in the profession seemed to be that public regulation was unnecessary. Little effort was made to license social workers. By 1965 only three states had licensing laws for social workers. Many workers and agency board members seemed to believe that the legal rights of clients were protected better by the values and ethics of the profession than could be possible through legalistic protections. Many social workers and their professional associations believed that their system of close supervision by colleagues was a more effective assurance of competent practice than any legal protections could ever be.

THE EMERGENCE OF A LEGALISTIC SOCIETY

Whether this view is valid or not is debatable, but there is little doubt about one thing—American society has become more legalistic and litigious. Professionals are scrutinized more heavily than ever; to an unprecedented degree they are held accountable, not only to their agency supervisors, but to their clients, their professional colleagues, and to the general public.

In the current climate of litigiousness, laws and rulings have been created to protect citizens against virtually every risk (Priest, 1990). When the risks have unhappy outcomes, professional practitioners are often named in lawsuits for malpractice. Social workers are not excluded from this circumstance; social welfare organizations, non-profit social agencies, and workers are being sued in increasing numbers (Macchiarola, 1988).

This trend seems to have begun in the early 1960s, starting with President Kennedy's message to Congress (Herrman, 1980). He proclaimed the existence of four basic consumer rights. These were: (1) the right to safety (protection against the marketing of goods or services hazardous to one's health); (2) the right to be informed (protection against fraudulent advertising or misleading information about products and services, and to be given the facts needed to make an informed choice in the marketplace); (3) the right to choose (reasonable access to a variety of producers and services); and (4) the right to be heard (assurance that consumers will get sympathetic hearings by all government agencies and that consumer laws will be enforced).

The consumer movement resulted in major changes in the way the helping professions provide their services. Professionals started advertising and overtly competing for clients. The various professional groups worked hard to define their respective turfs and proclaim exclusivity within that realm. All the professions helped legislators develop more stringent licensing laws.

Social workers left social agencies and the supervision of experienced colleagues and entered private practice where the only controls on their practice was through licensing and peer review. The omissions and commissions of public agency social workers, especially in making recommendations to legal authorities about clients, were intensely scrutinized by the legal system. Workers involved in child abuse cases, adoptions, custody disputes, marital mediation, parole, and commitment procedures were challenged in courts with increasing frequency. Mental health professionals were being held accountable in courts for failing to accurately predict violent behavior in their clients (Meloy, 1987).

SOCIAL WORK IN THE LEGALISTIC SOCIETY

In this climate, social work has had to renew its interest in the law. However, a closer integration between social work and the legal system is far from complete. To achieve it, social workers still need to improve their knowledge about the law. Correlatively, opportunities for them to obtain increased knowledge and sophistication must be improved. The professional schools of social work still have few course offerings in legal aspects of practice. Professional conferences devote relatively little attention to such concerns (Barker, 1989). The social work literature is still predominately oriented to clinical and social policy issues with comparatively minimal space devoted to the law. And there still seems to be considerable sentiment within the profession to deal with clients "humanistically" rather than "legalistically" (Miller, 1990).

Nevertheless, the progression continues. Legal regulation of social work practice now exists in all jurisdictions of the United States (Landers, 1992). Social workers are called upon by courts of law to provide expert testimony, with increasing frequency (Patru, 1989; Gothard, 1989a). They are also being called to courts of law to defend themselves against criminal negligence and malpractice charges (Besharov, 1985).

Furthermore, the schools, professional conferences, and social work literature are gradually reflecting the new circumstances. At least a dozen schools of social work now sponsor joint MSW/JD degree programs with law schools, although enrollments are low (Brieland and Goldfarb, 1987). The number of elective courses in graduate schools has increased, although there are few required courses. Professional conferences have tried to increase their presentations and workshop offerings in this field. For example, the most recent (November 1990) NASW professional conference keynote speaker was social worker-judge Sol Gothard, who discussed the need for increased integration of social work and the law.

The available literature is reflecting this need. Several good books about the law and its relationship to social work and other **helping professions** have been published in recent years (Schroeder, 1982; Besharov, 1985; Brieland and Lemmon, 1985; Albert, 1986; Curran et al., 1986; Thyer and Biggerstaff, 1989; Brown, Unsinger, and More, 1990). Many of the social work journals now include legal issues with regularity. Nevertheless, this is still small compared with the amount of print devoted to health/mental health and to the social problems of individuals.

THE EMERGENCE OF FORENSIC SOCIAL WORK

Because the societal trend is compelling a closer relationship between law and social work, the time is propitious for the development of forensic social work as a systematic field of practice. With such a historical, if interrupted, alliance it is surprising that such a field has so far remained underdeveloped.

Forensic social work can only develop when several steps are taken. Individual workers, as they continue to encounter the growing influence of law in their profession, need to become more knowledgeable about it. So, too, the social work professional associations must give more recognition to this situation and more opportunities for members to learn about it.

Members of the Council on Social Work Education and other social work educators could encourage more courses with legal orientations to be offered in accredited professional schools. Some of these courses could be made into requirements rather than electives. More field placements in legal settings such as family and juvenile courts, private law offices, public interest law organizations, and legal aid and community law centers would also be useful. Giving greater emphasis and publicity to the joint law/social work degree programs would be productive. So, too, would be encouraging social workers who have experience in expert testimony to make presentations to colleagues.

Social work also could delineate what is to be included in the specialized forensic social work field of practice. The fields of both law and social work encompass so much about human society that this specialty could easily become so broad as to be meaningless. Thus, it is important to be specific about the functions that are integral to forensic social work. So far, ten activities could be included in this specification. There is considerable overlapping of these functions, and additional ones are sure to be added in the future.

TEN FUNCTIONS OF FORENSIC SOCIAL WORK

First, the forensic social worker provides expert testimony in courts of law. In this role the worker provides requested information in general about the human welfare needs of individuals, families, groups, and communities. For example, the worker might disclose what usually happens to the personalities of children or wives who are abused. Expert testimony is also given to legislative committees and lawmakers so they can decide if people need a new law or not.

Second, the forensic social worker systematically evaluates individuals so that the resulting information can be presented in court or to legal authorities. These evaluations are conducted to answer many questions that the court needs to know, such as the following: In what way has this person been psychologically and socially damaged by the defendant? Why did this person behave this way? Is this person responsible for his actions? What happened in this person's background which helps explain his current behavior? Is this person competent to stand trial?

Third, the forensic social worker investigates cases where criminal conduct has possibly occurred and presents the results to judges, juries, and other law authorities. For example, the worker testifies about visits to the home of a family whose child has been physically and sexually abused.

Fourth, the forensic social worker recommends to courts of law and other legal authorities ways to resolve, punish, or rehabilitate those found guilty of crimes or negligence in civil actions. For example, after evaluating a defendant to see how he is likely to react to various punishments, the worker delineates to the court various needed community service projects that could be fulfilled by the defendant that would be useful in his rehabilitation.

Fifth, the forensic social worker can facilitate the court ordered sentence for the convicted person. This happens in many ways, but primarily involves monitoring the person and reporting any progress to the court. It also happens by providing treatment to the person or advice to those who work with the person. For example, the worker can actually supervise the convicted person as he or she carries out a community service sentence, or give advice to the staff at the site of the sentence on how to deal with the person. Social workers also function in the formal role of probation or parole officer in many jurisdictions.

Sixth, the forensic social worker mediates between individuals and groups who are involved in disputes or conflicts that might otherwise require extensive intervention in the courtrooms. Many people, especially couples with marital problems, want to avoid the adversarial nature of legal proceedings and do so through professional mediation services. This has become a burgeoning field in which social workers are very active, especially in those states that encourage the mediation process. Mediators must be well versed in the law as well as in aspects of human nature in order to help disputants find fair and enduring resolutions to their conflicts.

Seventh, the forensic social worker testifies about the professional standards of social work to facilitate cases of possible malpractice or unethical conduct. When a social worker is sued for malpractice it is necessary to establish in the court what the standards are that were violated. Both the defendant and proponent attorneys might call upon social workers to describe specified elements of the profession's code of ethics and other professional standards. Social workers might also be asked about whether certain practices are the most efficacious or safe and whether other procedures might have been preferable. Such information might also be sought in peer review investigations and when the professional organization has a committee on inquiry to determine if a worker has deviated from professional standards.

Eighth, forensic social workers devote considerable attention to educating their colleagues about the influence of law on their profession. They teach courses and give workshops on the legal aspects of social work practice. They provide consultations to agencies and individual workers about how to provide professional services within the law and with respect to the risks of liability. In a variety of formats they inform colleagues about the causes of malpractice and professional sanction. They also inform lawyers and other legal officials about social welfare and the social work profession.

Ninth, forensic social workers facilitate the development and enforcement of licensing laws to regulate professional social work practice. They help develop these laws, educate the public and the profession about them, and help assure that they are continuing to meet the needs of the public, the clients, and the members of the profession.

Tenth, and most important, forensic social workers maintain relationships with their own clients which uphold the letter and spirit of the law and the ethical principles of their profession. In this respect at least, every ethical and competent social worker has become a forensic social worker.

WHAT SOCIAL WORKERS NEED TO KNOW ABOUT THE LAW

To fulfill these functions competently, most social workers will need to learn more about the legal system. They will need to know about how laws are made, changed, interpreted, and enforced. Knowledge about courtroom procedures is also essential. Forensic social workers should be very knowledgeable about general procedures in courtrooms, grand jury settings, judges chambers, and law offices. They need to know what the roles are of the various persona involved in trials, and this knowledge should be based on serious study rather than watching television courtroom dramas or serving on jury duty.

Regarding information that they give to legal officials, forensic social workers must know about admissibility of evidence, that is, what information is and is not considered admissible in court. In this context the worker must know how to obtain accurate information from clients, legally and ethically, so that it can be considered as admissible evidence. And of course the forensic social worker should be knowledgeable and polished as to the presentation of effective testimony.

Social workers also need to know about malpractice exposure. They need to know its causes, and all the behaviors that a worker can perform which have led to suits. They need to know how to avoid such behaviors and to minimize the negative consequences of legal action, for their own sakes and for the well-being of colleagues or clients whom they are helping in such actions. Forensic social workers may serve on either side of malpractice cases, so they need to know how to present their viewpoint in ways that strengthen the case upon which they are working.

In dealing with clients in a litigious society, social workers need to know how to maintain relationships that meet the client needs while minimizing risks of misunderstandings or conflicts. Contracts which spell out the goals and procedures of the therapeutic relationship can be prepared for the signatures of both client and worker.

Social workers should also become knowledgeable about what the law requires of them in their work with clients. Workers are not always fully informed or aware of legal requirements or changed laws. Some social workers still do not know, years after such laws were made, that they may be required to report their suspicion of child abuse or threats their clients make to harm others.

Forensic social workers need to know about the legal regulation of the profession and other forms of accountability. Licensing, peer review, third party review, and professional scrutiny and sanctions, are all increasingly important considerations in social work practice. When workers have problems with reviewers or licensing regulators they are likely to seek the services of colleagues who are knowledgeable about such matters, i.e., forensic social workers.

CONCLUSION

The following chapters discuss each of these aspects of social work and the law. The intent is to present an introductory outline about the various issues instead of an exhaustive detailed presentation. Each issue presented here includes a list of the most important references available in this new field. The bibliography at the end of this volume contains the essential literature of forensic social work. To read all or most of these books and articles would give the social worker a good foundation in the knowledge of forensic social work.

Also at the end of this volume is a short glossary of the legal terms that are used herein and which are most likely to be used by social workers in their professional encounters with the legal system.

Chapter 2

Presenting Testimony
as an Expert Witness

Providing useful and relevant information to legal officers, judges, and juries is becoming a more important social work role than ever. Social workers have unique access to information that judges and juries can use to make fair decisions and good laws. The most frequent use of social workers in courts pertains to such issues as child abuse/neglect cases, custody, rape, and sanity determination (Spakes, 1987). They provide this information by testifying as expert witnesses according to established procedures in courts of law.

Effective performance in the role of expert witness is challenging and complex. Doing it well requires considerable knowledge, experience, and social skills. The requisite knowledge includes courtroom procedures, admissibility of evidence, and the roles of the participants in court cases, as well as the specific information requested. Experience is important because it enables the worker to respond to the examiner's questions in ways that are most helpful to all concerned. Social skills are important in giving the worker the ability to clearly communicate the information without being diverted or distressed by the manner of questioning.

THE ROLE OF THE EXPERT WITNESS

When legal decisions are reached, the process is usually facilitated by people who present relevant information, that is, witnesses. There are several types of witnesses, depending upon the type of information to be presented. These include the "lay witness" or "fact witness" (one who testifies, not as an expert, but as a direct observer of the events being presented), the "character witness" (one who testifies as to the reputation of an individual involved in the case), the "material witness" (one whose testimony is so essential to the case that it cannot be concluded without it), and the "expert witness."

The expert witness presents background information to the court about the issues being debated or adjudicated. This information is usually not about details of the specific case but about general facts and educated opinions and hypotheticals regarding situations of this type. For example, the social work expert may describe to the court what the latest scientific findings are regarding the well-being of children who are removed from the home of one parent and placed in the home of the other. Or the expert may describe the ethical and professional standards of the profession and what treatment methodologies would be most appropriate for a given type of condition.

Court decisions or laws are rarely reached solely as a result of the expert witness's testimony. Rather this information is used to establish the context or framework within which to view the actions of the individual(s) being tried. Most malpractice and other civil suits, and many criminal cases, utilize expert testimony for this purpose. The expert witness has special knowledge which is not possessed by the average person. This knowledge is usually derived from formal education, study, or experience. The role of the expert witness is to explain, to teach, and to elucidate matters beyond the ordinary layperson's ability to understand.

QUALIFYING A WORKER AS AN EXPERT WITNESS

In order for the expert's knowledge to be presented in court, the party producing the witness must qualify the witness as an expert. This party (usually a lawyer for either the plaintiff or defendant) also must establish that this particular case requires the use of expert testimony. This requirement occurs when the fact finder (frequently the jury but in many cases also the judge) needs assistance to understand or evaluate the evidence.

The expert can be excluded from giving testimony when the judge and jury do not need assistance to understand or evaluate the evidence. It can also be excluded when it invades the province of the jury or judge. This can happen when the witness's information relates to the ultimate issues or conclusions in the case. This is true even though modern evidence rules may permit testimony as to ultimate facts or conclusions, at least in theory. Judges, however, resist. They naturally resent the expert whose testimony attempts to wrap up the entire case for one side or the other.

WHY SERVE AS AN EXPERT WITNESS?

Expert witnessing has become a booming business for specialists, including forensic social workers. It can be financially and professionally rewarding for the professional who is well-prepared for the role. If not well prepared, providing expert testimony can be a most unpleasant and costly experience.

In presenting expert testimony, experienced forensic social workers believe they fulfill their professional function of facilitating social justice, maintaining the benefits of the social order and helping to eliminate social problems. Through this role they also help protect vulnerable individuals, and they enhance their own profession and the other mental health professions by revealing to law authorities what the standards of good care are.

The expert witness role has some personal rewards too. Of course there is gratification in being publicly recognized as an expert with unique knowledge and perspectives. Payments received for this work can be considerable, and it is a refreshing respite from one's normal activities.

However there is a downside. The worker's credentials and professionalism may be challenged by the opposing attorneys or advocates. They are likely to ask what social work is and whether it is a profession with the specific expertise for the particular case. When confronted by opposing attorneys in depositions or on the witness stand, the worker will likely face caustic questioning and cross-examination. The worker may encounter some ridicule or legalistic tactics designed to diminish the effect of the testimony or shake the witness's confidence.

The social worker will probably need to set aside a considerable amount of time for the process while waiting for the actual court appearance. Witnesses must be available to go on the stand at any moment, but no one can predict when that moment will come. The witness cannot watch the trial so it is usually necessary to wait in hallways or witness rooms. Most cases are settled out of court, often just before the trial begins, so much of this waiting seems to serve no purpose. Most experienced witnesses advise taking a book or some work so that the wait can be more productive.

Other disadvantages to presenting expert testimony are serious but do not occur in all these cases. When testifying in malpractice cases, one naturally will have the enmity of a colleague and all the colleague's supporters in the community. And finally, it sometimes is a challenge to collect the fees agreed to by the attorney and client.

PREPARATION AS AN EXPERT WITNESS

Some of the disadvantages can be minimized with careful preparation. This includes learning as much as possible about the case itself and the issues surrounding it. It also includes understanding general litigation discovery and courtroom procedures, and especially the law of evidence. Knowing what type of evidence can and cannot be admitted is helpful as is knowing how to frame answers during examinations by counsel. This knowledge can be acquired in advance of work on a specific case by reading, reviewing testimony given by other experts, attending trials and legislative committees, and talking with experienced attorneys.

Of course, one cannot prepare for a specific case until asked. Attorneys locate their own expert witnesses as part of their planning on the case. They often find them through referrals by other attorneys, or by reviewing similar court cases in which the expert participated. Sometimes they find them through reviewing the literature or by calling nearby universities. Attorneys also call the professional associations in the area for input on who the recognized experts are. Social workers who make public or media presentations on the subject are also frequently sought (Schultz, 1991).

Once an attorney asks the social worker to participate as an expert witness, the worker's specific preparation begins. The first step in this preparation is for the worker to decide if he or she can, in good conscience and comfort, support the position desired by the attorney who makes the request. Then the worker must also decide if he or she can be of actual service or help to the client's case. Once the worker feels comfortable about being able to provide the service with competence, the next step is to make a firm agreement with the lawyer.

The lawyer is hiring the worker to perform a service, so the worker needs to know the conditions of employment. The worker needs to know what information will be sought, how much time it will take, how long the case is expected to endure, and how the fees will be paid. The worker should not agree to serve as an expert witness unless these points are established through a legal contract with the attorney.

RECEIVING PAYMENT FOR TESTIMONY

Many conflicts between attorney and expert witness can be avoided if a firm agreement, that is a written contract, is negotiated in advance. Many cases take years to resolve and most are settled out of court. Most civil actions are financed on a contingency basis, i.e., the attorney gets paid only upon winning the case. These circumstances place the witness in a vulnerable situation and the lawyer might be unenthused about paying. They could say: "We didn't win so we have no money to pay you." "We settled out of court so you didn't testify and thus shouldn't be paid for something you didn't do." "Because your credibility was challenged and the judge refused to hear your testimony, you didn't deserve payment."

To avoid such problems, the worker should never agree to payment contingent on the outcome of the case. Moreover, a contingent payment arrangement would altogether destroy an expert witness's appearance of detachment and credibility should the opposing attorney bring that fact out in cross-examination or deposition.

Instead, the agreement or engagement letter should indicate that fees will be paid on an ongoing basis within 30 days after the bill is submitted to the attorney. Some experts charge a retainer or engagement fee against which time will be billed. Others specify that all or a portion of the retainer will not be refunded should the case be settled quickly. Because the expert witness is the attorney's employee, payment is the responsibility of the attorney, not the attorney's client. It can be very difficult to get payment from a client after the case is resolved, no matter what the outcome.

If the worker's services are no longer needed at any point during the case, often because of settlements, the fees incurred up to that time should be paid immediately. Even without actually making a court appearance, the expert's presence is often influential toward getting the opposition to agree to a settlement. In any event, the worker should seek all payments due prior to sharing the findings.

Generally the fees for this service are based on the time actually devoted to the case. Most experts charge the same rate per hour for this work as they normally charge in their other work, and which is customarily charged by their colleagues for such work. Otherwise they could be depicted in court as having mercenary or vested interests in the cases. They should charge for all the time they spend on the case, including travel time, time spent waiting in courthouses, and time spent in research, interviews with those involved in the case, and planning testimony. Charges are also made for all relevant itemized expenses such as transportation fares and secretarial costs.

SERVING AS FACT WITNESS OR EXPERT WITNESS

When social workers are asked to testify, it may sometimes be unclear whether they are fact witnesses or expert witnesses. The expert witness is supposed to answer hypothetical questions which are closely based on the case's actual facts and which the expert will have carefully examined. The fact witness is supposed to answer questions about what was actually seen or experienced. A worker cannot be both in a given case.

The blurring of roles may occur when a worker conducts an examination of someone who becomes a participant in a case. The worker could be asked about what the subject said or did during this examination rather than being asked for a general opinion about the subject.

If a worker is seen as a fact witness by a party to litigation, the worker can be compelled by subpoena to testify in trial or deposition. A pure expert witness may not be compelled to testify, or may be compelled only with great difficulty. This can be an important financial consideration for the worker who would only be paid if in the role of expert witness.

GENERAL AND SPECIFIC KNOWLEDGE NEEDED

Once the worker agrees to serve as an expert witness, it is time to learn as much as possible about the specific case. Of course this begins by asking the attorney for information about the facts of the case, the kind of information sought in the testimony, the procedures and personalities of those involved in the case, and any other pertinent information.

The worker should investigate the case thoroughly by reviewing all relevant documents, previous decisions, and relevant legal actions. If the worker is being asked to interview a subject of the trial, professional ethics apply to the interview procedure just as much as to any other professional work with a client. Whenever possible these interviews should be videotaped, beginning with the initial contact. This is to show the court, when necessary, that the information gleaned from the subject was not due to the interviewer's influence.

It would be useful for the worker to prepare notes about the case, and include therein such factual data as relevant dates and places, names of the important people involved, and information about any diagnoses, symptoms, and historical data. This material usually can be brought to the trial and referred to if the worker has any difficulty remembering it.

Many expert witnesses help to prepare themselves through rehearsal. After reviewing the case and discussing with the attorney the questions they will be asked, they write out all possible questions and answers. Then they try delivering these answers orally, duplicating as much as possible what and how they will present themselves in court. Others recommend against such preparation, saying that the result would seem stilted and insincere and that opposing attorneys can easily trip up one who has programmed answers. Each witness must decide what is personally the most comfortable and effective manner of presentation.

It is also important for expert witnesses to know the limitations of their expertise. If these limitations are recognized and acknowledged to oneself and to the court there be less of a tendency to go beyond the information possessed. When an expert does this it is usually discovered during cross-examination. The entire presentation loses much of its credibility.

PROCEDURES IN PRESENTING ACTUAL TESTIMONY

One of the most unpleasant aspects of the expert witness role is the long waiting, often in relative isolation. Witnesses might wait for days before their appearance is called for. They are frequently sequestered from other witnesses or participants in the trial in order to ensure that their testimony is not colored by the testimony of others.

When finally called and sworn in, the witnesses first identify themselves, their occupations, and the nature of their expertise. This is sometimes called "qualifying the expert" or "laying a foundation." At this point the attorney may formally move that the court accept the social work professional as an expert.

If accepted by the court for the information they have to present, experts are first questioned (direct examination) by the lawyer who employed them, known as the proponent, and then by the opposing lawyer (opponent) in cross-examination. Sometimes after the cross-examination the proponent may ask additional questions (redirect examination), followed by recross-examination, or surrebuttal. After the testimony is completed, the court may allow the witness to remain in the public gallery if there is no further need for testimony. Otherwise the worker has no further involvement in the case.

The expert witness will have some influence on the case outcome depending upon the amount of credibility (i.e., believability) established. To be a credible witness, the worker should appear to be confident, comfortable, and knowledgeable about the case and respectful of the court and its procedures. The worker should be dressed appropriately (usually in a business suit) and act in a professional manner. Showing respect for both attorneys as well as the judge and jury is important as is presenting an appearance of objectivity, impartiality, and recognition of one's limitations. One should never convey disapproval with the judges's rulings either in verbal or physical expressions.

Answers to the lawyers questions should be stated as simply and jargon-free and slang-free as possible. Answers should be concise, responsive, and relevant specifically to the question asked. It is essential to listen carefully to the question asked and to be sure that the question is understood before an answer is offered. Some experienced witnesses make it a practice to always pause before answering, even to the extent of mentally counting to three before speaking. The witness should avoid to the extent possible any vague responses, or personal/emotional conjectures such as "I think that. . ." or "I feel. . . ."

DISTINGUISHING FACTS FROM OPINIONS

The witness should avoid giving opinions or drawing conclusions, unless they are specifically requested. The "Opinion Rule" in courtroom procedures requires witnesses to limit their testimony to the requested facts without the embellishment of opinion. The opinions of expert witnesses are sometimes admitted but are usually limited to matters of which the witness has the expertise or personal knowledge. Moreover, the opinions they express must be clearly derived from the existing facts.

However, there are some exceptions. Sometimes ordinary witnesses are asked for opinions within the competence of ordinary observers, such as whether a person seemed to be drunk, or driving faster than safe, or physically or mentally ill. Modern schemes of evidence permit, or no longer authorize exclusion, of experts' opinions on the grounds that they relate to or resolve ultimate issues or conclusions in the case. Nonetheless, the judge may exclude the expert's conclusion about ultimate facts on the grounds that the testimony is just too prejudicial to the other side.

In any event, it is essential that the expert witness preserve one's sense of integrity and appearance of detachment or objectivity. The witness must never let the attorney put words into his or her mouth. The witness should never take a position on an issue unless it is the product of his or her own informed professional judgment.

The information offered by the witness must be considered by the court to be relevant, material, and/or competent. Facts that are relevant are those which relate to what the lawyer is trying to prove.

Material evidence is that which has important bearing on the case. Competent evidence is admissible because it is relevant, material, and capable of shedding light on the issues being litigated. The expert witness will not have too many difficulties separating fact from opinion by keeping statements in this sphere.

However, the expert witness can sometimes run afoul of the issue about "hearsay evidence." Hearsay evidence is legally defined as an out-of-court declaration sought to be admitted into evidence to prove the truth of the matter asserted by the declarant. Generally the hearsay rule says that evidence is not admissible unless it comes directly from the declarant in court. Because the expert witness is often asked about what others have said or revealed, the problem about hearsay can exist. Usually hearsay evidence is excluded because the subject did not make the statement under oath and is not available for cross-examination. Furthermore, the statement may have been made in a different context than the use to which it is put in the court. Nevertheless, there are numerous exceptions to the hearsay rule. These should be discussed thoroughly with the lawyer prior to testifying. Because the lawyer must establish a basis for attempting to include such information into the court record, the worker will not bring it up without having worked it out with the lawyer first.

TACTICS OF OPPOSING ATTORNEYS

The most difficult experience for many workers in the expert witness role is in the cross-examination. The opposing lawyer's basic objective during cross-examination is to challenge the credibility of the information presented. This is done by questioning the witness's credentials, pointing out inconsistencies, revealing gaps in the witness's knowledge, and trying to show that the witness is not reasonable or objective.

Experienced cross-examining lawyers have an arsenal of tactics that may be used to undermine the expert's credibility. They may ask leading questions, use intimidating countenances, and attempt to make the witness feel vulnerable to charges of wrong doing or incompetence. Phrasing questions in such a way that the witness cannot give proper answers is another tactic.

Leading questions are those which suggest the answer the questioner desires, and those which evoke responses advantageous to the questioner. Leading questions are generally not permitted on direct examination but are permitted on cross-examination, which affords greater latitude. If an attorney objects to a question as leading, the judge will decide whether to allow it. If not allowed the examiner will be required to rephrase the question or ask a new one. The expert witness should answer such questions only when it is required by the judge.

Some lawyers favor attempts to intimidate the witness. This is frequently done by affecting a tone of hostility, sarcasm, ridicule, or by asking questions that suggest some wrongdoing by the witness. The attorney may ask questions such as, "How much are you being paid for this testimony?" or "What were you told to say?" Obviously the worker has discussed the case with others and is probably being compensated, and no one in the courtroom construes it as wrongdoing. But if the questions causes the witness to seem evasive, apologetic, or angry, the attempt to weaken the worker's credibility has worked.

A favorite approach used by opposing attorneys to undermine the witness's credibility is by asking questions that cannot responsibly be answered. For example, the lawyer will demand a "Yes or No" response when a detailed explanation is the only way to convey the information. Technically, a lawyer cannot demand a simple "yes" or "no" under these circumstances. However, unless the opposing lawyer comes to the witness's rescue, the witness may be forced to answer in this way.

In a similar tactic the lawyer asks a question that is stated in a long, confusing manner that is more a speech than a request for the information. The witness is vulnerable to an appearance of confusion or uncertainty in such circumstances. When this happens, the witness is cautioned to wait for the opposing attorney's objection, or to ask for the question to be clarified before attempting an answer.

The opposing lawyer's tactics will work to a greater or lesser degree, depending on how capable the witness is in response. The effective witness will provide a service to the cause of justice and will likely be asked to appear at future court hearings.

TEN GUIDELINES FOR THE EFFECTIVE WITNESS

To make an effective presentation as an expert witness the following specific guidelines are suggested:

1. Always answer every question truthfully, including those for which the correct answer is, "I don't know."
2. Answer the questions succinctly, clearly, and confidently.
3. Avoid emotional responses or overreactions to hostile questions.
4. Do not answer anything other than the question asked; do not volunteer additional details or irrelevant facts.
5. Do not take personally the examiners' questions, brusque manner, or hostile approaches. They are just doing their jobs.
6. Before answering any question, pause to deliberate about the answer; avoid getting caught up in the examiner's rapid-fire questioning which can lead to confusing or inaccurate responses.
7. Do not prolong the time before answering; undue delay will seem like uncertainty or dishonesty.
8. Pause briefly after each question to permit the attorney to object without revealing information that would not be admissible.
9. Stop immediately when an objection is made; proceed thereafter only when the judge rules on the objection and/or provides instructions to continue.
10. Always remain calm and polite with both lawyers, judge, and all others present; never argue with anyone about their questions, procedures, or rulings.

Chapter 3

Malpractice and How to Avoid It

Malpractice occurs when a professional person causes harm to a client through improper performance of duties. It does not matter whether the professional's conduct is intentional or occurs through carelessness or ignorance. A competent and ethical social worker might think, therefore, that the risk of malpractice will be minimal. Social workers assume that if they adhere to the highest standards of the profession, conform to the professional code of ethics, conduct treatment competently in accordance with the traditional methods of the profession, and always achieve what are considered successful therapeutic outcomes, there would be no problems with malpractice.

A worker who believes this nowadays is naive. Most competent professionals would be hard pressed to say they have always been able to accomplish these results. But even if they did, they could still be vulnerable. Consider the following examples of actual cases.

SOME MALPRACTICE EXAMPLES

A 19-year-old man has just been medically discharged from the U.S. Army for depression after three months in the Saudi Arabian desert. He returns to his parent's home and they urge him to seek treatment. He seeks help with the Veteran's Administration but finds that the waiting list for help is too long. So he begins working with a social worker at a family service agency. After four months of therapy he shows signs of considerable improvement. He gets a job, makes new friends, and many of his depressive symptoms are diminished. He then decides he wants to get a place of his own. He decides to stop therapy to save money.

The worker advises against it, saying that the depression is likely to return, and the therapist and agency even agree to reduce fees to assure continuing treatment. The man does not keep the next few scheduled appointments. The worker calls several times and is told by the young man that he no longer wants to come. The therapist never sees him again. Three months after the last session the young man commits suicide. His parents, feeling that the therapist did not do everything possible to anticipate or alleviate the suicidal tendencies or either keep him in treatment or get him hospitalized, seek compensation from the worker though a lawsuit.

A middle-aged woman is a victim of the "learned helplessness syndrome." Married to an abusive alcoholic for 18 years, she has a high paying job and is the family's sole source of support and stability. She has been unable to get her husband to work on his problem or stop his abuse. Nor has she been able to get out of the marriage, primarily because of severe problems of self-destructiveness and insecurity. At the encouragement of her Al-Anon group she enters psychotherapy.

The therapy helps her to become self-confident, less self-destructive, and determined to improve or end the marriage. After presenting an ultimatum to her husband, to get help or get out, the marriage comes to an end. The husband then explains to his divorce attorney that the therapist caused the breakup of the marriage and ended his source of livelihood. The therapist is then sued for the loss of income and other harm he has allegedly caused the husband.

A woman has been in a private social work practitioner's group therapy for several months. She is an attractive young mother of two, in treatment because of conflicts about her sexuality. She confides to the group that she recently broke off a secret affair with a married man. Another group member is very interested in the woman's revelations. With severe characterological problems he has had various troubles with the law, difficulties holding jobs, unsuccessful relationships with women, and deep-seated resentment toward authority.

Even though everyone in the group is admonished to honor and respect each other's confidentiality and to not see one another outside the group, the man secretly starts following the woman to her home after group sessions. He calls her on the telephone. She rebuffs him and calls the group therapist. The therapist contacts the man and reiterates the group rules about confidentiality and no outside contacts. The man becomes enraged at the therapist and refuses to continue his sessions. The woman also refuses to return to the group, despite the therapist's attempt to get her to continue. The man now begins calling the woman and harassing her. He threatens to reveal her secret to her husband and to her ex-lover's wife if she does not meet with him. When she still refuses, he writes letters to both families. This results in a considerable conflict between spouses. They all seek legal assistance and attribute much of the blame for their troubles to the group therapist. They contend that the therapist should not have included the man in the same group with her and should have exercised more control over the man. The therapist was forced to defend against threats of litigation from two parties.

It is easy to see how the most well-meaning and competent social worker can become enmeshed in malpractice litigation. In all of these examples the workers were highly capable and experienced, yet they had to defend themselves against blame for events over which they may have had little or no control. As is true of most malpractice cases, all of these were settled before reaching the courtroom (Barker, 1982). Nevertheless, the workers had to expend considerable funds, time, and energies to defend themselves, and their reputations could never be fully restored.

RESPONSIBILITY FOR THERAPY OUTCOMES

These cases became malpractice issues, not because the workers' behaviors were incorrect, malevolent, or unusual, but primarily because the outcomes were so unhappy. Yet many clients do not achieve successful results no matter how competent the therapist is or how reliable the methods usually are. The first case illustrates the difficulty of predicting the risk of suicide. While professionals can identify the signs that are most commonly associated with suicidal ideation, many people who take their own lives do not show such signs in advance (Ivanov, 1987). Moreover, even when they do, it is not possible to hold people against their wills for long.

The second example illustrates that some people might be unhappy with the consequences of the therapy even when the outcome is "successful." It is not uncommon that therapy leads clients to make changes in their lives which negatively impact others. If these others perceive that they have been harmed by the professionals' work, they can initiate legal actions.

The last case illustrates the vulnerability of professionals who are sometimes seen as being responsible for client behaviors. If the client causes harm to another, those harmed wonder why the therapist did not do more to prevent such actions. This view has become so prevalent in our society that laws now compel professionals, in certain circumstances, to take actions to protect others from their clients.

While society increasingly holds professionals responsible for the behaviors of their clients, the authority of professionals to control their clients is diminishing. It is rarely possible to keep clients in therapy or custody against their wishes, no matter how much they might need it. The social trend is to protect the rights of mental patients against the actions or controls of therapists. Therapists cannot make clients take their needed medications, cannot incarcerate when clients do not seem imminently lethal, and cannot accompany them through their lives to protect those with whom they interact.

CRITERIA FOR MALPRACTICE LIABILITY

Of course most malpractice cases occur as a result of a worker's actions that are clearly outside the standard of professional conduct and are directly harmful to the client. Malpractice occurs when a professional causes harm to the client through a lack of care or skill. Unlike the ordinary person on the street, a professional is held to a certain minimum level of skill or competence. The law holds that the professional should bring to the task at hand that amount of skill and knowledge possessed by the typical professional within the same discipline in the same or similar communities.

To recover damages in any malpractice action the plaintiff must prove four elements: (1) that the professional owed the client a duty to conform to a particular standard of conduct, (2) that the therapist breached that duty by some act of omission or commission in the professional practice, (3) that the client suffered actual damage, and (4) the professional's conduct was the direct or proximate cause of the damage (Bernstein, 1978).

To win a malpractice case, the plaintiff has to establish that all four of these elements existed. The first element is the most clear-cut. A duty of care is established if a worker/client therapeutic relationship has already begun, especially if verbal or written contracts have been made and fees have been paid for the service.

Establishing the third element, that the client has suffered actual damages, is also clear-cut, although more complicated. It is difficult to show emotional damages as a result of what social workers and other mental health professionals call "talking therapy"; it is not so difficult when the client develops health problems, commits suicide, is improperly incarcerated, or harmed physically. The plaintiff's attorney will attempt to establish damages by documenting the client's health and circumstances prior to and after the therapy. The documentation will probably include medical case records, physicians' testimony, and other witnesses' testimony about the client's condition before and after the professional's intervention.

Most malpractice disputes center on the other two elements: whether or not the worker's care met established standards and, if not, was that substandard care related to the damage. To ascertain this in court, the plaintiff's attorney will call on expert witnesses, members of the defendant's profession if possible, to explain what the standard of care requires for cases of the type experienced by the plaintiff. This may include testimony from social work practitioners, educators, and members of the professional association and licensing authority.

The evidence presented most certainly will include a review of the social worker's code of ethics. Behaviors by the social worker which are at variance from this data will be noted. The plaintiff will not likely prevail if the defendant can show clearly that the practices were in accord with professional standards or that the professional made an acceptable choice of treatment alternatives from a range of acceptable choices.

However, most cases of this type do not reach the courtroom when the defendant can show that these standards were reached. Many plaintiffs gain de facto victories when defendants settle out of court, paying sums to avoid the considerable inconvenience and notoriety that would be faced by contesting the case in court.

If the court determined that the worker's care was substandard and that the client was damaged, it theoretically becomes necessary to link the two. In practice however, the plaintiffs' attorneys are sometimes successful when they simply establish that damage was done and that the worker's care deviated from standards. It is easier to get a jury to make the connection as its members tend to sympathize with a damaged client than with a successful professional.

DEFENSIVE OR PREVENTIVE PRACTICES

The defendant does have some defense however. To rebut proof or inference of proximate cause, the defense could attempt to show that some other person's action superseded any alleged negligence by the defendant. Thus if the plaintiff had gone to other professionals after working with the defendant, it becomes more difficult for the jury to decide where any negligence might lie.

While there are no guarantees against losing malpractice cases nowadays, the practitioner's best hopes are in always adhering to professional standards of conduct. This means that the worker must first know what those standards are. Ignorance of the standards is in itself practicing at a substandard level. Next, the worker must choose to meet those standards. Most of the known claims against mental health professionals have been made in situations where the professional knew what was appropriate and inappropriate conduct but chose the inappropriate action anyway.

Unquestionably, the best defense is to avoid going to court at all, by convincing the plaintiff or the plaintiff's lawyers that they cannot win a favorable judgment and will not receive a favorable settlement. Preventive practice, while not guaranteeing the avoidance of litigation, can reduce its likelihood to the extent possible.

To achieve this goal the worker needs to maintain an explicit rationale for every action taken. This rationale should be documented in writing in the client's case record. Then, when the plaintiff's lawyer reviews this record and finds a full explanation and justification for the course of action taken, the plan to proceed with the case becomes very daunting for the plaintiff. Then the worker must remain knowledgeable about the specific types of malpractice litigation that befalls colleagues and avoid such conduct.

SPECIFIC CONDUCT LEADING
TO MALPRACTICE CLAIMS

The specific conduct that leads to malpractice claims has been delineated by social work professional associations and by insurance companies which underwrite malpractice coverage. The largest of the companies for social work malpractice insurance is the American Home Assurance Co. They periodically report on the number and type of claims received from social workers and agencies in various categories (American Home, 1987).

The following number of claims have cumulatively occurred for each specific type of alleged professional misconduct:

Incorrect treatment...................................78
Sexual impropriety 69
Breach of confidentiality...........................46
Improper child placement 41
Improper diagnosis or faulty assessment 31
Defamation.......................................28
Improper death of client 26
Failure to supervise client properly...................23
Bodily injury to clients 22
Violation of civil rights...........................21
Suicide 21
Countersuit due to fee collection 19
Assault and battery 17
False imprisonment 13
Breach of contract 11
Failure to warn of client's dangerousness...............9
Failure to cure, poor results 6

Many other isolated activities, not categorized here, have also been listed by the insurance company. While most of these actions have not reached courtrooms, all of them have required the social worker to engage legal representation and develop defenses. This in itself is a costly and inconvenient process which every worker wants to avoid. The balance of this chapter discusses these types of claims and offers some suggestions for avoiding similar fates or minimizing the consequences when they are not avoided.

Incorrect Treatment

The professional conduct that results in the highest number of malpractice claims is providing the wrong type of treatment for the client. "Wrong treatment" cases are most likely to occur when the worker's therapy causes damage by keeping the client from receiving more appropriate treatment. The following case illustrates:

A 34-year-old man is referred to a social worker by a friend who had previously been successfully treated by the worker. For six months, the man had been taking three five-milligram tablets of Valium daily because of anxiety. He tells the worker that the tension seems to have begun in the past year and is increasing. It becomes so severe, he says, that his heart pounds and he sweats profusely. He attributes his symptoms to the growing pressures of his job and to some unresolved conflicts about the death of his mother two years ago. He assures the worker that his last physical examination was normal and that he had no health problems. After treatment begins, catharsis seems to help. The client has a marked diminution of the anxiety symptoms. But after three months, the symptoms return and seem to get worse. The worker recommends increasing the number of visits to twice weekly. Again there is a reduction of symptoms for awhile, but then they return with even more intensity. One day at work the man becomes so upset he is taken to a nearby hospital. Tests follow. The consulting physicians discover that the symptoms are not caused by functional neuroses, as was assumed by the worker. The diagnosis was "mitral valve prolapse syndrome."

Such diseases result in many of the same symptoms as seen in people with severe anxiety disorders; yet the treatment for each is far different. It is not possible to know if behaviors that seem like anxiety are due to inner conflict or to medical disorders by merely talking with a client. Therefore, the appropriate standard of care and defensive practice is as follows: **Before commencing therapy,**

require the client to get a physical examination to rule out medical causes of presenting symptoms.

Sexual Misconduct

The second most common conduct resulting in malpractice claims occurs when social workers engage in sexual relationships with their clients. It seems probable that there are many more common forms of professional misconduct than sexual intercourse with clients, but those forms of misconduct are more difficult to substantiate or to recognize as misconduct. There is less room for mistaking client-worker sexual contact as acceptable practice, so litigation is more likely to occur whenever it happens.

Even so, many therapists try to justify their action as something other than inappropriate conduct. In such actions, many defendants claim they ended the formal therapy sessions before actually engaging in such liaisons. At one time a common defense was to claim that such behavior was therapeutic and not-harmful to the client, and that it was not that much a deviation from the standards established by well-known leaders in the psychotherapy fields. This argument has waned in recent years as every reputable professional indicates (and will in courtroom testimony) that there are no valid justifications for sexual relationships. Some leaders in the field, such as Masters and Johnson (1970), say it should be treated legally as the crime of rape.

All mental health professions' codes of ethical conduct now include specific prohibition against sexual relations with clients. The social work code of ethics, for example, says very simply but clearly: "the social worker should under no circumstances engage in sexual activities with clients." But what constitutes a client? Is there a point in time after which the person is no longer a client and thus eligible for such a relationship? Hopefully the benefits of therapy are lifelong; the influence of the therapist exists equally as long. Thus, one never leaves the status of "client." Therefore the defensive practice is this: **Once therapy has begun, a sexual relationship between the therapist and client is permanently inappropriate.**

Misuse of Influence

In addition to sexual misconduct, some therapists have induced client behavior that serves the professional's rather than the client's interests. For example, misuse or undue influence occurs when therapists persuade their clients to include them in their wills. It also exists when a therapist convinces clients to sell them property, especially without giving proper remuneration or other adequate consideration.

The relevant standard is clearly explicated in the social work code of ethics. It says, "the social worker should avoid relationships or commitments that conflict with the interests of the client." The obvious precaution here is as follows: **Avoid any social, financial, or any other relationship with the client that is not explicitly therapeutic.** This standard remains in effect permanently too. There is no way of knowing that the influences which the worker has developed with the client during the course of therapy will not endure for life.

Breach of Confidentiality and Defamation

The appropriate standard of care is for the therapist to say nothing about the client to others without the client's written permission. The principle of confidentiality has always been regarded very seriously by social workers. Careless disclosures to outsiders about information obtained in formal interviews are rare. However, circumstances exist in which confidentiality and defamation problems occur even though the worker's intentions are honorable. The following case illustrates:

Several months after Mr. Jones successfully concluded his treatment with the social worker, he went up for promotion in a highly sensitive government agency. His applications indicated his recent therapy. Mr. Jones signed release of information forms so that the employer could obtain additional information about the therapy. In the face-to-face meeting with the employer's agent, the worker gave little information and tried to emphasize only the positive aspects of the client. However, the investigator became suspicious about the social worker's minimal responses. Later the agency asked Mr. Jones to sign another release to obtain the worker's entire case record. The records contained information that was not positive about Mr. Jones. He did not get the promotion. The therapy and its record were the only factors to account for denial of the promotion. In a malpractice suit, Mr. Jones alleged he was harmed because of the information given by the worker, information that would not have been revealed if the worker had been more circumspect with what he wrote in the case records.

Cases such as this have been disputed between mental health professionals and their clients for many decades. Possibly the most famous was the *Yoder v. Smith* case (Slovenko, 1968), in which a doctor was asked by a patient to send information to the employer; the information showed that the patient was unable to perform some of his former duties on the job. While this case was ruled in favor of the plaintiff, most are not. This is because the argument the defendant makes is that the allegedly harmful statements were not lies and had been solicited by the plaintiff. However, many more cases of this type are settled before they reach courtrooms. In these instances the settlements more often favor the plaintiff, as the defendant agrees to make some payment to avoid the negative publicity, legal costs, and loss of time. This was what Mr. Jones' therapist did.

The relevant standard of care and preventive action is this: **Do not disclose any information about clients without the client's written permission. Do not put anything derogatory about a client in the record.** Many professionals also recommend that in preparing case records, the client participate in its writing and receive copies of everything written. This means that the worker will usually be more careful about what is written. If anything is written that is distressing to clients, therapists and clients can discuss it in the therapy office rather in than the courtroom.

Faulty Diagnosis or Assessment

When social workers investigate conditions in which children, older people, disabled persons, and others are living, they usually report this information to legal or medical officials for appropriate action. When that information leads to the client being placed inappropriately, and when the decision to do so was based on the worker's input, malpractice liability is possible.

One of the most expensive settlements made by a social worker to date was over this issue. She evaluated a client and prepared a report for a psychiatrist to use in court. The report said the client was not dangerous. Soon thereafter the client shot several people, including himself. Both the psychiatrist and the social worker became involved in extensive and prolonged litigation. They eventually settled a large claim out of court to avoid further litigation.

The standard of care and preventive defense here is as follows: **Maintain accurate and complete records based on information from as wide a source as possible. This record should include information about how it was obtained and disclaimers about possible inaccuracies therein.** Judgments about placing clients must be made with as much input as possible from colleagues, other professionals, the client, those in the client's environment, and those in the environment where the client may be sent.

Death/Suicide of Client

The death of a client, either through unsupervised accidents, untreated health problems, or suicide, is the most serious and visible form of damage. So, while death of a client may not occur with frequency, when it does it is very likely that legal inquiries will ensue. The authorities and attorneys of the family will want to determine the degree, if any, to which the therapist might have precipitated the results.

When professionals are investigated for client deaths, the experience is more painful than merely being concerned about malpractice litigation. The therapist will feel saddened by the client's death, but due to the nature of the relationship cannot express grief as can family members. Moreover, the therapist will often feel somewhat responsible, even if there is little connection between the therapy and the death. Finally, while the therapist copes with these emotions, it is important to prepare for a defense.

Workers are sometimes burdened with contradictory expectations in society. On the one hand, they may be expected to know, at all times, if their clients are suicidal or in jeopardy of self-injury. Yet, when workers suspect that clients are in danger, they are limited in the extent to which they can incarcerate or otherwise control the client. For one thing, to do so places them at risk of malpractice through faulty assessment and violation of the client's civil rights. The standard of care and defensive practice is this: **Know all the signs of suicide ideation, medical symptoms, and the likelihood of the client being unable to avoid accidents. When any of these signs are observed, close monitoring is crucial. When protective incarceration is unfeasible, then enlist the client's family and other associates in the monitoring process.**

Failure to Defer or Refer to Other Professionals

Part of ethical treatment of clients is for the worker to provide whatever services are needed and to refer to other appropriate professionals whenever the needs are outside the worker's expertise. The referral should be made to a reputable professional who is properly trained to provide the service needed. Malpractice litigation often occurs when a worker fails to see the need for referral, or if referrals turn out to be harmful to clients.

In the exercise of reasonable care, the professional standard is well established. Social workers must tell their clients whenever they know (or should have known) that their forms of treatment will not or might not be effective, and that more effective treatments are available than the workers are trained to offer. The referral practices that are common in the same or similar community or state weigh heavily in this standard.

For example, if a client suffers from anxiety or depression, the therapist must nowadays consider medication first. It may be recommended as the sole method of treatment for the anxiety, or in connection with psychotherapy. Only after it has proved unsatisfactory, then the longer, drawn-out form of insight therapy or behavioral modification techniques alone may be used. This means that physicians must be consulted for this condition, because only they can prescribe medications. And if there is any doubt about the nature of the condition, the physician should also be consulted.

The nonmedical psychotherapist should consider psychiatric consultation whenever there is a question of which type of treatment to use. The therapist could be liable to malpractice claims if he has not had some form of consultation with a physician about the client and the client is thereby damaged (Bernstein, 1978).

If a social worker treats a client who requires medical care in collaboration with the therapy, the worker must be careful not to encroach on the physician's activity. One case illustrates how this is so. In 1990 a social worker was found criminally guilty for dispensing medicine (Valentine, 1990). The worker shared offices with a psychiatrist and helped with the psychiatrist's patients. Often after an initial visit by the physician, the worker would virtually take over the case, writing prescription renewals and ordering medical tests in the name of the physician. Both the worker and physician lost their licenses, were placed on probation, professionally sanctioned, and had to pay heavy fines for their actions.

The relevant standard of care and defensive practice should be obvious: **Social workers should know their professional limitations and stay therein. They should refer their clients appropriately for any needs that go beyond those limits.**

Premature Termination

Problems concerned with ending the treatment relationship are also a source of potential malpractice liability. If the worker requires the client to stop, even though the need for help continues, the worker may be responsible for subsequent harm to the client. Workers sometimes want to discharge clients who are still in need because the client's funds or insurance coverage have been exhausted. This is of dubious ethics and legality. There must be an orderly and professionally prescribed process by which the client discontinues therapy. If the need continues, and the client is adhering to the contract, the worker must continue or facilitate a suitable referral.

The professional standard of care indicates that treatment must continue until one of three conditions exist: both therapist and client agree to end it; the client explicitly and unilaterally decides to conclude; or the therapist decides to conclude because the client no longer needs service. Therapy ends only when one of these conditions is met, but there must be some documentation to demonstrate that such is the case. When written contracts have been utilized at the beginning of the therapeutic relationship, termination processes may be expedited. In any termination it is wise to put the decision in writing, with a summary letter or a termination of treatment notice.

Sometimes the client forms a transference-based attachment to the therapist, or the therapist feels attached to the client through countertransference. These feelings cause the treatment to extend beyond the point at which treatment is still productive. If the client wants to continue because of the attachment but is not in need, the worker must use care to terminate without making the client feel rejected or personally abandoned. Sometimes if the treatment seems no longer productive, the worker should acknowledge the fact and refer the client to another professional for treatment or a "second-opinion" consultation.

Some workers have recognized that their clients do not need continued therapy but continue seeing them to collect fees. Some therapists collect reimbursement fees from insurance companies for services supposedly rendered after the client has stopped the sessions. Civil malpractice and criminal actions have ensued in such instances.

The standard of care regarding termination is this: **Discontinue treatment only after needs have been met or the client has been appropriately referred.**

Treatment Without Informed Consent

Many other malpractice conflicts would be averted if the worker develops a relationship with the client that is based on informed consent. In any therapy the client must agree to the service offered. The client must consent willingly and explicitly to any treatment methods to be employed. Voluntarily entering therapy is usually considered implied consent. Signing a written contract that spells out the goals, procedures, risks, alternatives, and rules would be explicit informed consent. Only when the client is unable to consent because he or she is a minor or judged legally incompetent because of mental illness or other incapacity is there likely to be a consent problem. In such instances consent is obtained from the parent or the person legally responsible for the client, such as a *guardian ad litem*.

Malpractice damages can be awarded if the client was not properly informed about the methods to be used. Lacking disclosure, any consent the client has given is not "informed" consent. For example, if a client has a misperception about the nature of treatment and is not told about the methods before undergoing them, the therapist may be held liable for any resulting damages. Some clients may have been led to expect that positive results are a certainty; clients sometimes expect positive results to be achieved in a very short time at a minimum of cost. A claim could be upheld unless the therapist could prove that no assurances, guarantees, or claims were expressed or implied. Lack of informed consent also occurs when a worker has not warned a client about the limits of confidentiality and is then compelled by law to disclose some information to authorities that was revealed in the interview.

The most problematic aspect of this is the failure to advise clients of the risks or dangers that might occur in their treatment. There are some risks in any treatment and, of course, the client has the right to know this. If adverse effects subsequently occur, and if the client had not been warned of the possibility, a court could rule against the therapist. So the standard in this instance is as follows: **Before therapy begins, provide the client (or the client's legal guardians) with adequate written information about the course of treatment proposed, possible alternatives, and risks or dangers each treatment may pose.**

Failure to Warn

Social workers and all other mental health professionals face a dilemma. Generally, they are required to respect client confidentiality. But the law also requires them to protect the public if the client constitutes a danger. Malpractice claims are increasingly made against social workers who have failed to warn either the public or intended victims when their clients have indicated their dangerousness. The decision made by the Supreme Court of California in the *Tarasoff v. Board of Regents* case presents one horn of this dilemma. The effect of this decision is to require therapists to warn those who are threatened by their clients. However, the duty of confidentiality and the solid justification for it forms the other horn of the dilemma.

Malpractice claims have been upheld against social workers who failed to warn intended victims. But so too have claims succeeded when social workers have issued such warnings and the client has not subsequently harmed anyone. Charges of defamation as well as breach of confidentiality are then made. The fundamental conflict between two contradictory ideals, and a resolution of that conflict is the focus of the next chapter.

Chapter 4

When Laws and Ethics Collide

A Chinese proverb says, "Whether a stone hits a jar, or a jar hits a stone, it is the jar that is broken." So, too, when the law and a professional's ethics are in conflict — it is always the ethical position which succumbs.

For the most part, such collisions should not occur. Professional ethics should not be contrary to the laws of the jurisdiction in which the profession is practiced. Law exists for the maintenance of society and protection of its citizens. As such, law has precedence over the rules, codes, or statutes of self-regulating groups within that society. When considered as an abstract generality, this view seems unquestionable. And in fact, most ethical principles held by a profession are consistent with the relevant laws. The most glaring exception, however, is that of the principle of confidentiality.

THE LIMITS OF CONFIDENTIALITY

In social work, as well as all the other helping professions, this principle was held to be inviolable until recent years. It was considered unethical to reveal what a client said in the therapeutic interview. Professional practice wisdom taught that effective therapy could never occur if the client feared disclosure. Violators of this principle were sanctioned by the profession and subject to legal action as well. Clients were reassured that they could say anything without fear of adverse consequences.

However, changes in the law in the past 20 years have dramatically altered the principle of confidentiality, for some professions at least. While clergy and lawyers can still assure their clients that they will not disclose confidences, mental health professionals cannot. Laws now compel social workers and other professionals to report suspected child abuse, neglect, and threats by clients to harm others. Accordingly, the Codes of Ethics of social work and the other helping professions have been rewritten. The NASW Code of Ethics no longer says that client confidences are to be maintained but that "the social worker should share with others confidences revealed by clients, without their consent, only for compelling professional reasons" (NASW Code, 1991).

CHILD ABUSE AND NEGLECT LAWS

A series of state and federal laws were enacted in the 1960s and 1970s, culminating in the federal Children's Justice and Assistance Act, effective October 1, 1986 (Saltzman, 1986). These laws generally require that social workers, teachers, physicians, and other professionals are to report suspected cases of child abuse or neglect to designated authorities. Criminal and civil liability may be imposed on those failing to comply.

Workers who observe or infer from indirect signs that the child is being abused or neglected are required to notify law enforcement authorities promptly. The grounds for reporting suspected child abuse or neglect, as summarized by Besharov in his important 1985 publication, are as follows: Direct evidence, such as (a) eyewitness observations of a caregiver's abuse or neglect, (b) finding the child in physically dangerous circumstances, (c) the child or caregiver's own descriptions of such behavior, (d) demonstrated inability by the parent to care for a newborn, and (e) disabilities by guardians that are so severe that they are not likely to be able to provide needed care.

Indirect or circumstantial evidence, according to Besharov, includes such concerns as (1) suspicious injuries suggesting abuse, (2) supposedly accidental injuries that show gross inattention to the child's safety needs, (3) injuries or medical findings suggesting sexual abuse, (4) signs of severe physical deprivation, (5) extremely dirty and unkempt home, (6) untreated injuries, illnesses, or impairments, (7) unexplained absences from school, (8) apparent caregiver indifference to the child's severe emotional or developmental problems, suggesting emotional maltreatment, (9) indifference or approval by the caregiver of the child's misbehavior, and (10) abandoned children.

To bring professional standards into compliance with child abuse legislation, the National Association of Social Workers issued its standards for social work practice in child protection in 1981. Standard 38 states: "The Social Worker Shall Comply with Child Abuse and Neglect Reporting Laws and Procedures: It is the responsibility of every social worker to obtain knowledge of the state's child abuse and neglect laws and procedures, and to share this knowledge with employers and colleagues. In addition, whenever it is necessary to report a case of suspected child abuse or neglect, the social worker shall collaborate with the local office of Child Protective Services as appropriate, shall explain the report and the CPS process to family members" (NASW, 1981).

Many legal and professional conflicts followed the institution of child abuse-neglect laws and professional guidelines. Workers who have reported their suspicions which subsequently could not be legally substantiated have been fired, demoted, sued, and tried in criminal courts (Besharov, 1983). So, too, have been workers who failed to report abusive situations even though they may have had no way of knowing that actual abuse had taken place.

"DUTY TO WARN" LAWS

The law also requires social workers to disclose confidences when their clients reveal intent physically to harm others. Court decisions or statutes in many states compel mental health professionals to report such findings to authorities and/or intended victims. Of course there is little provision in the law to protect workers if they report such information and no harm actually ensues. Professionals have been successfully sued and fired for making such assertions.

A fundamental premise of psychotherapy is that the client verbalizes thoughts and emotions to understand them better. Through this the client gains control over impulses that might otherwise be overwhelming. So the client comes to feel trust in the therapist and freedom to disclose all thoughts, no matter how strange or socially unacceptable they might seem.

By no means is it unusual for clients to fantasize about wanting to harm others, or cathartically to dissipate anger by describing feelings rather than acting upon them. However, when social workers are forced by law to reveal such verbalizations, such thoughts are far less likely to be expressed. If the feelings are felt, but not expressed and worked through, or if the client avoids therapy because of the fear of disclosure, the problem remains. Clients, both potential and actual, as well as therapists and society, may be at greater risk since "duty to warn laws" have been instituted.

THE TARASOFF CASE

To understand how such laws came to be made we must review the case that started the "duty to warn" requirement. The now-famous *Tarasoff* decision was authored by the Supreme Court of California in July, 1976. A University of California student named Tatiana Tarasoff decided to stop seeing another student she had been dating. The young man was so disturbed about her decision he entered therapy at the University Counseling Center. In the next few weeks, he told his therapist of his anger about Tatiana's rejection, and of his growing urge to get even. Eventually he told the therapist he planned to kill her.

Many questions ran through the therapist's mind. How serious was the threat? Most clients make such statements in therapy at some time or other. If this was a serious threat, what could be done with the young man? Commitment or imprisonment were unlikely solutions. The young man was not psychotic and no crime had yet been committed. Police constantly tell people who are threatened that they really cannot do anything until an actual crime has occurred. Even if arrested, the young man could not be held indefinitely. And after being released, would he ever want to see a therapist for help again? Should Tatiana and her family be warned? If nothing could be done anyway, it might be needlessly upsetting to them. If they are warned and nothing happens, would the therapist be liable for defamation?

After discussing the situation with the supervisor, the therapist decided that confidentiality was less important than a person's potential safety. The campus police were notified and they picked up the young man. They interrogated him about his relationship with Tatiana and of his stated plans for murder.

The young man minimized his threats. Yes, he said, he had been upset in the clinic. Sure, he told his therapist, he was angry enough to kill Tatiana, but he was just letting off steam, like the therapist told him to do. He was convincing and the police released him. Soon after that he carried out his threat and murdered Tatiana.

The parents brought legal actions against those involved in the case, including the therapist, the supervisor, and their employer, the University of California. They wanted to know why the police had been warned, but not the family. They believed that if they had known of the danger, they could have taken preventive measures and their daughter would still be alive. After many trials and reversed decisions, the case reached the state Supreme Court.

Ultimately, the judges decided that the therapist's actions were improper. It was not enough, they concluded, that the therapist had notified the supervisor and authorities and even attempted to have the student incarcerated. Because he and other university officials had reason to believe the client was at large and dangerous, the "failure to warn Tatiana or others likely to apprise her of the danger constituted a breach of the therapist's duty to exercise reasonable care to protect Tatiana" (*Tarasoff v. Regents*, 1976, p. 2d).

IMPLICATIONS OF THE TARASOFF RULINGS

Social workers and other mental health professionals across the nation have often been confused about the decision and its obvious consequences (Simmons, 1981). It meant that henceforth therapists had to notify others, usually including people they had never met, that a client seemed likely to do them harm.

This became the law in California and eventually in most other states. The ruling was authored by the highly respected Judge Roger Traynor. Judge Traynor's influence with other judges and lawmakers was so great that his opinions tend to be adopted by his colleagues. Judges throughout the nation have used the Tarasoff decision as precedent in reaching similar conclusions.

These rulings have been applied to everyone who provides direct counseling or psychotherapy in all settings, whether institutional or private. This includes psychiatrists, psychologists, social workers, pastoral counselors, marital therapists, probation officers, and many others, and their supervisors as well (Reamer, 1989). Supervisors who advise against such disclosures may share the liability even though supervisor liability does not absolve the direct practitioner from responsibility.

The *Tarasoff* decision is now a major influence in the way counseling and psychotherapy takes place in the United States. Obviously, when clients are told that what they say may be reported to authorities, they are going to be cautious about their words, but not necessarily their deeds. Yet therapists must tell every client, at the beginning of therapy, of the limits of confidentiality.

If therapy is undertaken and the therapist does not make the client aware of these limits, the therapist has failed to procure informed consent to treatment. And, as we have seen in Chapter 3, failure to procure informed consent is a form of malpractice in most jurisdictions.

CONFUSIONS AND CONTRADICTIONS

Even when clients are informed about these issues many uncertainties face the worker. The requirements and criteria for reporting are unclear and often inconsistent. The purpose of these requirements is ultimately to protect society and some of its more vulnerable members, but unless the criteria for reporting are clear, protection is not certain.

The confusions result in many questions that must be answered: How should the intended victim be warned in such a way that it is not so alarming that the resulting upset itself constitutes a danger? How does the worker fulfill the ethical obligation to help the client through to termination, after such disclosures have been made? What does the worker do if the client continues in therapy after disclosures and makes threats against other people too? If the disclosure results in incarceration for the client, what is the criteria for the client's eventual release? How long after the incarceration period will the client be considered dangerous? What are the criteria of dangerousness? Why should physical harm be the only threat that should result in disclosure? What protection does the law provide for workers against defamation actions when such disclosures have been made and proven to be unfounded? What should supervisors do when their workers report these concerns? If clients later deny they made threats in the worker's office, how far should the worker go to pursue the issue thereafter? Are Constitutional prohibitions against self-incrimination relevant? Can a client be confined indefinitely after making such assertions, when no crime has been committed?

THE RATIONALE OF JUDGES AND LEGAL OFFICIALS

Even though the requirements to disclose are troublesome and confusing for workers, judges and legal authorities have arrived at their decisions for good reasons. According to Judge Sol Gothard (1991), who is also a trained social worker, sound and logical reasons dictate why judges fashion these requirements for practitioners. For example, judges always make their decisions after the fact, after someone has been harmed. Moreover, they assume the worker is competent enough to know when a person actually is dangerous to others. And they see the professional's responsibility as including helping to maintain the social order.

Judges and lawyers assume that specific harm could have been prevented if the therapist's knowledge had been shared. After someone has been victimized by a therapist's client, it seems just to reasonable and socially compassionate people that the victim should have been protected. Failure to do everything possible to protect the vulnerable person naturally seems irresponsible to social workers; to judges and to victim's families, it also seems to constitute fault. Unfortunately for the worker, however, there is no certainty that a dangerous situation exists before the crime has actually been committed. The worker does not necessarily have knowledge that harm will take place, but only that the client has expressed such thoughts.

When judges rule that social workers should have warned intended victims when danger seems imminent, judges are assuming that workers can make such predictions accurately. Perhaps judges and others ascribe such prescient powers to therapists because of the effective public relations campaigns that therapists have conducted in the past decades to certify their worth. However, many studies show that therapists have no particular abilities to predict client behavior (Ennis and Siegal, 1982). Some studies have even indicated that therapists' predictions about dangerousness are more often wrong than right (Simmons, 1981).

The major collision of law and professional ethics occurs when judges view therapists as having a social control function. Representing society and the justice system, judges must be attuned to the rights of all citizens to be protected from individuals who intend to do them harm. Social workers and other therapists, on the other hand, tend to be oriented to helping the individual client to overcome current problems. Therapists see their primary purpose as helping the individual so that he or she will not want to harm others. Perhaps too readily social workers want to achieve this with the client independently of the controls legal and social systems impose. Whatever they may want, therapists must recognize that the social control function is an important and inescapable part of their responsibilities.

GUIDELINES FOR COPING

In conferences about the collision between legal and ethical responsibilities, social workers invariably ask for specific and practical guidelines for resolving these issues. They are usually unhappy to learn that the decision about how to respond to such problems is left to them. Every case is unique; it must be dealt with on an ad hoc basis. What a professional person is supposed to do with a possibly dangerous client before a crime occurs is different from what a professional should have done after the crime occurs. A professional person must make professional judgments rather than follow clearly detailed sets of prescriptions.

Nevertheless, the professional can take some precautions and actions. First is that workers must inform all their clients about the limits of confidentiality in order to remain free of "informed consent" liabilities. The client should be told at the outset that in cases of suspected child abuse or danger to others it will be necessary to inform authorities. This is best done in writing. An example of how this might be written appears in the next chapter on the written contract.

If then, during the interviews the client strongly indicates an intent physically to harm someone, the worker must warn the client of the consequences. Inasmuch as there will be far more times that a client makes a threat than actually carries one out, the worker cannot immediately issue warnings. But if the client persists in such remarks, the worker should try to get the client to communicate the threat to the intended victim. Letters or phone calls made in the presence of the worker can help fulfill this responsibility.

If the worker believes that the client is not actually dangerous, but wants to minimize the probabilities of any problems without issuing warnings, considerable therapeutic attention to the issue is in order. For example, the advice might be for the client to look at the grievances more objectively, and to get away from the other person for a cooling off period. Getting rid of any lethal weapons is imperative. Sometimes procuring the client's consent to attend a meeting with the other party in the therapist's office is a possibility. Any other therapeutic actions that can help the client look at the other person in a less threatening manner should also be taken.

IMPLEMENTING THE ACTUAL WARNING

If, however, such therapeutic activity does not have the desired effect, and if the worker is convinced that the client continues to be serious about the intent to harm someone, some systematic procedures for issuing the warning must be taken. Ideally, the disclosure should be made generally with as much input from the client as possible. If the client cannot or will not inform the other party about such feelings, then the therapist must do so. It must be done fairly promptly too, because some judgments have found professionals liable for not making the notification early enough.

To whom should the therapist make the disclosure? This varies from one jurisdiction to another. Social workers should first notify any of their own supervisors or employers. Then, in most cases, the most appropriate division within the local police department and the office of the relevant county prosecuting attorney should be called. If the case involves suspected child abuse or neglect, the professional should also contact the local office of Children's Protective Services (or equivalent name in some jurisdictions).

To these authorities, the worker simply says something like, "I'm a licensed social worker in your jurisdiction. I'm working with a client who has said (s)he intends to harm someone. The law in this state says I must report this to you and I told the client a few minutes ago that I am going to do this." The authorities receiving such a call will ask questions at this point, all of which should be answered completely and truthfully. The worker should then be available to the authorities at a moment's notice.

Whether or not the notification was tape recorded, the worker should immediately write notes describing what was said to whom. The names of those authorities receiving the call should also be listed. If the authorities misplace this notification the case could be treated as though notification was never made. After writing these notes the worker should contact the local professional association and/or office of professional licensing.

Unless the worker has reason to fear physical harm from the client, maintaining continued therapeutic contact can be worthwhile. Continued contact enables the therapy to continue; hopefully this can eliminate the impulse that led to the threats or otherwise resolve the problem. If the client is held by the authorities for questioning and arrested, the worker can do whatever is possible to see the client and maintain some therapeutic alliance.

Eventually, through this unpleasant ordeal, the intended victims will be apprised of the situation. It is better when the warning comes from the legal authorities rather than the worker. However, when this happens the people warned are then likely to contact the workers for further information. The client may also seek contact with the worker. The worker should not try to avoid the client or the other party; nor should the worker avoid the questions that will naturally be asked. However, these questions should be courteously referred to the authorities. The worker should be sympathetic with the intended victim but should not attempt to provide therapy.

If the social worker ascertains that the intended victim is in need of therapy, the worker may make a referral to another qualified professional. If the worker became the intended victim's therapist, **the original client could feel even more betrayed and angry than ever.** The client could feel there is collusion between the worker and the other party and could then easily transfer the feelings and intention to do harm to the worker. Many workers in such situations have been endangered and harmed (Schultz, 1989).

CONCLUSION

Social workers and other mental health professionals, without benefit of hindsight or powers of prediction, must frequently make judgments about potentially and actually dangerous clients. No single response can be best for all circumstances of these types. Social workers will always have to make professional decisions using their best professional judgment for each unique circumstance. So many variables in clients' personalities and circumstances exist, and differing legal interpretations compound the problem so as to preclude hard and fast prescriptions for dealing with these situations. Until the courts clarify and make more consistent their interpretations, the social worker will remain in a confusing situation.

Chapter 5

Using Written Contracts with Clients

A written contract is an explicit statement detailing the goals, procedures, obligations, and conditions for fulfillment by all the parties to the contract. In professional psychosocial therapy relationships, the agreement is entered into by the person(s) serving and the person(s) served.

The therapeutic relationship begins when the parties sign this contract; it concludes when all the terms and obligations of the contract have been fulfilled. The contract can be used to keep the focus on goals, and to minimize misunderstandings. If properly drawn and implemented, the contract will have considerable legal weight in malpractice or other law suits, or in peer review Committees on Inquiry (COIs).

WHY SOME WORKERS DO NOT USE WRITTEN CONTRACTS

Most social workers and other mental health professionals do not use written contracts with clients. One researcher (Barker, 1986) estimated that fewer than 20 percent of the social workers who are in private practice use written contracts, and far fewer in agency based practice use them.

A few professionals (Miller, 1990) argue strongly against the written contract, but most simply avoid the issue. When asked why, their answers vary. Some are afraid of them. They feel their clients would be offended. Some believe their agency-employer should assume this responsibility if it is to be assumed at all. Many do not want to be doing something they do not see most of their colleagues doing. They did not learn about contracting in their graduate

schools or field placements. There is little in the professional literature about contracts, and that which exists is mostly devoted to
discussions about the value and growing need for contracts without
specifically delineating their contents (Fatis and others, 1982).

Many workers avoid the written contract because they feel it will
cause them more malpractice and peer review problems than it will
solve. These workers reason that the legalistic nature of the contract
will diminish the attitude of mutual respect and will exacerbate any
tendencies to litigation. Statements in the contract will remind the
client of the essentially business-like nature of the helping process.
Pointing out in the contract that there are conditions in which confidentiality can be breached is distasteful to contemplate.

Perhaps the most important reason why many workers do not use
written contracts is that it seems to be alien to their basic treatment
model and professional orientation. Most psychotherapy providing
social workers consider themselves to be of the "psychosocial/sys-
tems" or "humanistic" orientation; they think of contracting as
being part of the orientation they oppose — the behavioral or task
centered treatment model.

CONTRACTING AND THE PSYCHOSOCIAL ORIENTATION

The humanistic and psychosocial orientations in social work interventions do not emphasize the establishment of goals at the outset of treatment. Inherent in these orientations is the view that the
human psyche is infinitely complex and the socio/cultural milieu in
which one functions is even more so. The professional's therapy
role is to guide the client through this complexity, gradually uncov-
ering and sorting out this material. When this point is reached, as
determined by the professional rather than the client, then the therapeutic relationship can come to an end.

Establishing specific goals at the beginning of the therapeutic
relationship is rarely done in this orientation. Workers believe it is
impossible to predict what new issues or problems will emerge during the course of therapy or how long the intervention will take. In
this view, the client is best served by relying, not on any explicitly

written set of mutual obligations, but on the worker's honesty, objectivity, ethics, and knowledge.

Often, if a client were to question the professional in any of these aspects, many professionals would probably interpret "resistance" or a "negative transference" problem. Such interpretations would mean that more time and money had to be expended by the client to deal with these issues even if they had not been relevant before therapy began.

The most prominent orientation that is opposed by the psychosocial/humanistic model has many names. These include "behavioral therapy" (Sundel and Sundel, 1985), the "functional school" of social work (Taft, 1936), the "problem solving school" (Perlman, 1952), and the "task-centered approach" (Reid, 1978). While these schools have essential differences from one another, they all define goals specifically, delineate means for reaching them, and identify the conditions in which the relationship will exist. They tend to be short-term and highly focused on their specific objectives. They advocate written contracts. Most social workers of the psychosocial/humanistic model believe these orientations force a "minimalist" approach to therapy, in which the professional is obligated only to meet the contract's conditions rather than considering client needs that go beyond these written terms. For example, a professional might stop seeing a client when the terms of the contract are completed, even though the client has revealed symptoms of new problems during the course of the intervention.

This contention is disputed by advocates of the contract. They point out that there is nothing inherent in the written contract that requires a professional person to terminate with a client when the conditions of the contract have been met. If and when new problems or symptoms emerge in the course of the intervention, it is a simple matter to revise the contract or prepare a new one. In fact, a properly drafted written contract indicates that the professional is obliged to adhere to the professional code of ethics, which precludes premature termination of services.

Despite objections by social workers of the humanistic and psychosocial orientations toward written contracts, there is a significant trend toward their use. Even psychosocial workers are beginning to accept them, if not for theoretical reasons, then for practical ones. The trend may be the result of four influences — the consumer movement, third parties, malpractice considerations, and the movement toward professional accountability.

CONSUMERISM AND THE WRITTEN CONTRACT

The first factor influencing the trend toward contracting comes from the consumer of psychotherapy services. Many social workers have been reluctant to ask clients to sign contracts at the beginning of therapy, fearing client resistance. However, most workers who use contracts find that clients are not offended but tend to be more relieved and confident about entrusting their problems with such a conscientious professional.

In a perfect world, where professionals actually would have all the answers and actually would hold their client's interests paramount, the idea of a contract to regulate the therapeutic transaction might be superfluous. However, such a world does not and has never existed. While professionals might think of themselves and their colleagues as being wholly beneficent and dedicated to their clients, the clients cannot be so sure. Potential consumers often hear about how clients are sometimes ill-served and often victimized by professionals. For them to enter into a therapeutic relationship solely on the basis of trust and hope, with no clear goals or time frame seems unwise. To do so is no more sensible than making payments on the purchase of a house for years with no deeds, mortgage papers, or documentation.

THIRD-PARTY INFLUENCES ON CONTRACTING

If the consumer movement has not led professionals toward explicating the terms of their relationships with clients, the third parties have. Insurance companies, managed health care programs, and government funding agencies have led mental health professionals to reconsider the value of written contracts. While third-party paying organizations do not require professionals to use written contracts, they do require many of the elements found in written contracts.

In order for third parties to reimburse the professional for services to their insuree, third-party payers require that professionals indicate their goals in treatment, the reasons for the procedures used, and the estimated time frame within which goals are expected to be achieved. They require the professional to make this assessment in the beginning of the treatment, or at least as early as the reimbursements are supposed to begin. They also require that the professional is licensed or certified in the relevant jurisdiction and adheres to ethical professional standards. When a professional meets all of these conditions with the third-party organizations, the professional has already fulfilled most of the essentials of a contract.

Unfortunately, many professionals give more of this information to the third party than to the client. They often withhold from the client information about the client's diagnosis, treatment plan, or procedures, or even information about the professional's credentials and background. They justify this by saying that such information would get in the way of the needed transference, cause the client to lose confidence in the professional, or focus the client's attention on such a narrow range of issues that the whole problem cannot be addressed. This view remains influential among social workers even though there is no empirical evidence to support it and substantial evidence to the contrary (Wodarski et al., 1982).

MALPRACTICE INFLUENCES ON CONTRACTING

The third influence toward contracting is the spectre of malpractice litigation. Written contracts significantly reduce these risks. As seen in the Chapter 3, the most likely causes of malpractice suits include lack of informed consent, improper or faulty treatment, breaches of confidentiality, and premature termination and abandonment problems. Each of these potential causes of litigation is minimized through the contract.

If malpractice litigation were threatened, a statement about the explicated goals, procedures, and explanations would be crucial. The written contract would show that the professional was adhering to procedures to which the client agreed. When a client agrees to the conditions, any possible claim about a lack of informed consent would be remote.

A particular malpractice vulnerability involves the worker treating a client whose symptoms are caused by some underlying health problem. As we have seen, if the physical health deteriorates and the client is made to think that the social worker's help is all that is necessary, a high-risk situation exists. However, if a written contract recommends that the client obtains a medical examination at the outset of treatment in order to rule out related physical health problems, an attorney may not be able to argue successfully that the treatment was faulty.

Confidentiality problems are also reduced through written contracts. The contract can include an explicit statement about the conditions under which confidentiality may have to be suspended in order to comply with the law in the relevant jurisdiction. If the client agreed to these conditions, it would be difficult to later make a claim of malpractice for breach of confidences.

The contract could also address the potential problem of premature termination or abandonment. Premature termination means ending the sessions even though the client's problems remain. It also applies to instances in which the ongoing client faces an unanticipated problem and cannot reach the professional or get proper backup coverage. This could happen, for example, if the worker has taken a vacation and has not provided coverage for the client, or has not given the backup professional access to the case record. A contract could tell the client what to do in such cases or what backup professional is available to contact. With this information available, the client can rarely argue a case for abandonment.

PROFESSIONAL ACCOUNTABILITY
AND CONTRACTING

When a professional social worker is called before a peer review committee on inquiry, the allegations usually involve violations of standards or ethics code. These committees want to know if the worker has made false claims, engaging in practices beyond the recognized expertise, or besmirching the good name of the profession by some conduct. The written contract can be useful in answering such questions and assuaging the concerns of the investigating bodies. The contract explicates the worker's credentials, background, procedures, and goals so that everyone knows at the outset what claims are and are not being made. Few reputable workers would be willing to put in writing blatantly false claims about their experience or expertise. It would be easy for the committee on inquiry to apprehend and apply sanctions on those who do. So the client, the worker, and the profession are all protected.

WRITTEN VS. VERBAL CONTRACTS

Many of the social workers and social agencies which do not use written contracts suggest that they use verbal or implied contracts. Workers say they reach agreements with their clients in their first meetings. In these meetings they indicate the conditions of the interventions, discuss the goals, and specify when termination should occur.

However, many deficiencies in the use of verbal or implicit contracts have been identified. The most significant is that the client is probably not in a position to understand what the terms of the contract are. Usually clients come for help at the time when they are distressed; they want to talk about their problems and end their pain. They are ill-prepared at the time of the first interview to divert their attention from their problem to examining all the elements that must be a part of the contract (Rhodes, 1977). If the first session is taken up with a discussion of the presenting problem, no time exists to discuss the terms of the contract. On the other hand, if all the elements that must be considered in the therapy transaction are reviewed in the first session, there is scant time to look at the problem.

Verbal contracts are subject to misunderstanding, misinterpretation, changing rules, and problems of proof. They require clients to remember what was said during the stressful initial interview about such things as confidentiality, the worker's credentials, the way to get insurance reimbursement, the goals, and the ways of reaching goals. And even if the client could remember, in times of dispute, malpractice claims, or peer review issues, how can any of this be documented? Putting it in writing affords this documentation.

The next chapter includes a prototype contract which has been used successfully. It can be modified or used as a guide for workers who want to prepare their own.

Chapter 6

A Model Contract for Workers and Clients

A written contract should be a simple and concise document that the client can understand without a lawyer's interpretation. It should contain information about generally what to expect in the therapeutic relationship. It should explain the worker's obligations to the client and vice versa. The written contract should tell the client what to do when the worker is unavailable. It should discuss how the sessions should terminate when the goals are reached. It should give the client some knowledge about the qualifications of the worker or agency. It should explain the required methods of payment and something about how to facilitate reimbursement with third party institutions.

ELEMENTS OF THE WRITTEN CONTRACT

The written contract should contain space for the goals of the intervention to be written by the worker and the client. Finally, the written contract should contain space for the signatures of the client and the worker, following a statement that the undersigned agree with the terms of the contract.

A worker could use several different types of written contracts, depending upon what kind of client-system is being served. A contract used for an individual adult will not be the same as one used for a couple in marital therapy, a member of a group psychotherapy program, a family, or a community. If a worker has a variegated practice with different client-systems, the worker should have several versions of a written contract for each purpose.

Contracts are more effective and user-friendly when written in the worker's own style of communicating and in non-"legalese" terms. The contract does not have to be called that, but rather can be known as a "letter of agreement," or a similar sounding title.

Even though legalese is minimized to the extent possible in the written contract, it may be advisable that the worker show the various versions to a lawyer before using them. Various state laws and interpretations might necessitate some changes in the worker's prototype contract. The lawyer can help to put the language in terms understood in courts of law.

There are many versions of written contracts. They can be easily produced, and modified, for every type of client, using computer and desk-top publishing technology. A simple and effective one is a document printed or typed on both sides of one sheet of legal sized (8 1/2" × 14") white paper. The sentences are printed in eight columns, about three inches wide each. The sheet is then folded three times, each fold occurring in the middle of the spaces between each column. This produces a document that is 3 1/2" × 8 1/2".

The front page contains only the worker's name, degree, address, telephone number, and a line indicating who the client can contact in emergencies when the worker is unavailable. The last page is blank except for GOALS printed at the top. This permits the client and worker to spell out the objectives of the intervention. When the contract is folded, only the front and back pages show. Usually the client tapes the folded contract with only the "goals" page showing, in a prominent place, such as the refrigerator door.

A PROTOTYPE CONTRACT

The following is a copy of a written contract used for years by the social work author for individual clients. It begins with the second page. A discussion about how the contract is presented to the client will follow:

LETTER OF AGREEMENT

Hello.

Welcome to my office.

I hope your time here is worthwhile. I'm giving you this letter now in order to answer some questions you may have. It will tell you what to expect out of our meetings and how we should work together.

Please go over this carefully. Feel free to ask me anything about it whenever you have questions. You are welcome to show it to others in your family or other professionals you trust.

At the end of this letter there is a place for us to sign our names. Signing means we agree with all the points in this letter. There is also space for us to write down the goals we hope to accomplish together. We can review these goals as we go along. We can change them any time we want, if together, it seems like a good idea.

Now, let's discuss what you and I should understand and do to make our meetings worthwhile.

SEE YOUR DOCTOR. Please get a physical examination from your personal physician as soon as possible. This is important to make sure that none of your problems are the result of physical health difficulties. Since I am not a physician, I cannot know if you might have physical health problems which might be related to our work.

It is a good idea that your family doctor knows you are going to be working with me. Please tell him/her as soon as possible. It is also important that I am informed about any work (s)he is doing with you. I especially need to know about any health problems you may have. Please ask your doctor to send me this information as soon as possible.

I think information about your work with me should be included in your doctor's medical record. Therefore, unless you say otherwise, I'll write to your doctor to describe your progress. These letters can be included in your medical chart if your doctor wants. You will be given a copy of these letters before they are sent. That way any possible corrections or things you feel should be left out or added can be done before it is sent.

TIME OF APPOINTMENTS. Each of our appointments is scheduled to last 50 minutes. I am usually able to begin promptly at the scheduled time. It is very rare that I'm late for an appointment. If it ever happens, I'll try to let you know in advance, even if the delay is just a few minutes. If we must begin late we will still be together for the full 50 minutes. If you arrive late for an appointment, we still have to end the meeting 50 minutes after it was scheduled to begin. The charge to you for these shortened meetings will be for the full amount. You will not be charged for a session if you cannot keep it and let me know at least 24 hours in advance. You will be charged if you fail to keep a scheduled appointment or do not notify me 24 hours ahead of time.

EMERGENCY MEETINGS. I will try to be available to you as much as possible. The telephone numbers on the front of this letter are attached to 24-hour answering machines and I monitor them closely from wherever I am. I will try to return your calls promptly. If I am away from town during vacations or professional meetings, I will let you know how to reach me by long distance telephone. Or I will have a qualified professional in the area return your call. Your case record will be available to that professional, unless you indicate otherwise. If you feel the need for help and cannot reach me or the other professional, please contact your family doctor.

STOPPING OUR SESSIONS. We should agree together when it is time for our meetings to end and for therapy to stop. We can do this in two ways. If you prefer, we can specify as we get started when our last session will be. Then, when the time comes, we will stop, unless we make a new agreement and set new goals. If we end this way our last meeting will include a final discussion and summing up about things to do in the future. Of course, we can resume sessions after that if you want. The second way we might stop is to decide as we go along. We might decide together to stop because we have reached our goals. Or we might decide we are not going to reach them. This is a possibility because I cannot guarantee that we will reach all of the goals we establish together.

It should be understood that you may, at any time, tell me you wish to stop, for whatever reason. I'd prefer it if you came in for one final session after that so we can have a summing up and discussion about the future. If you stop coming without letting me know in advance I cannot assume responsibility for your care and well-being after that.

COSTS. The charges for each of these 50-minute meetings is $_____. This amount is the same if you attend the meeting alone or with other members of your family. The charge to you is the same, if with your consent, I see other members of your family in your behalf. If we agree in advance to have meetings that are longer or shorter than 50 minutes, the charges will be based on the amount of time we are together. For example, if you have a 25-minute session the charge will be half that of a 50-minute session.

METHOD OF PAYMENT. You may pay by cash, credit card (VISA or Master Card), check, or money order. You may pay me or my secretary directly at the time of each visit. If this is not convenient we can discuss other possibilities such as monthly billing. If your bill has not been paid before the end of the month you will be sent a statement, itemizing the charges and showing the total balance due. This amount should be paid within 10 days after the month begins.

If you are having any financial problems that keep you from paying in this way, let's discuss it. We can make special arrangements if necessary.

INSURANCE. Your health insurance may help to pay these charges. You should find out by contacting your insurance company or agent as soon as possible. If they will help you pay my fees, please obtain the proper forms from them and give them to me. I will complete my portion of the form and return it to you, not your insurance company. After that it is your responsibility to submit the forms to your company. Ask them to send the money to you and not to me.

Your payment to me should be made on time even if your insurance company delays in reimbursing you. You should know that health insurance companies generally don't reimburse expenses they consider to be unrelated to health. That means some companies do not pay for things like marriage counseling, some forms of therapy, and educational counseling. Some companies will only reimburse you when your physician has referred you to me and is involved in your treatment. It is important that you find out about these things from your insurance company if you plan on getting reimbursed.

CONFIDENTIALITY. My profession and my professional ethics require me to keep everything you discuss here in the strictest of confidence. I have no intention of ever giving out any information about you to anyone unless you ask me to. I have no objection, however, to your revealing anything you want to anyone you want about our meetings.

I will audiotape or video-record some of our sessions only with your permission. If you permit me to record a session you may have a copy of the tape if you supply a blank cassette. I keep a written record of our contacts. These notes help me stick to our goals. It also helps us get started where we left off last time. These notes are confidential, but I believe they are your property as well as mine. You may read these notes whenever you want and you may have a copy.

There is one possible exception to the principle of confidentiality. It applies to me and all other mental health professionals in this state. In some very rare circumstances I could be called upon (subpoenaed) to testify about you in court. This could happen if there was reason to believe I knew of certain types of criminal wrongdoing. Also if you indicate to me seriously that you intend to harm someone, I may be required to take action to prevent that harm from occurring, including alerting the authorities and/or warning the person who is being threatened. My colleagues and I are also required to report any suspected child abuse. In such situations my records about you could also be reviewed in court. If the law ever required me to do this I would try to discuss with you beforehand any testimony I might be compelled to present. Again, the likelihood of any of this happening is extremely rare, but you deserve to be informed of the possibility.

MY BACKGROUND: You are also entitled to know about my qualifications to provide service to you. I have been in private practice in this office since _____. Before that I worked at _____. I am also on faculty of _____, where I teach courses in _____. My profession is social work and I specialize in _____. My academic degrees are _____ from _____ University. I have been licensed in this state since _____ and am a member of the following professional associations: _____.

OUR AGREEMENT: You are the boss and I am working in your interests. You determine what your goals are and my role is to help you reach them. I may show you how to define your goals or show you what the consequences of reaching these goals might be, but you have the last word on this. On the back of this letter we will list the goals we hope to achieve in our work together. We both agree they can be changed any time. If we change goals we agree to restate them on another letter like this one.

SIGNATURE: We the undersigned have read this statement, understand it, and agree with its terms. We will comply with all the points in this on our personal and professional honor. It is understood that our relationship may discontinue whenever these terms are not fulfilled by either of us.

(signature and date)   (signature and date)

PRESENTING THE CONTRACT TO THE CLIENT

The most effective way to use the contract is to present it at the end of the first session. Others have recommended that the contract be presented during the first session (Seabury, 1987) but doing so greatly diminishes the time available to concentrate on the client's problem. If used at the end of the session, the worker can incorporate it into a discussion about the goals.

Usually the worker will take some time at the end of the session to suggest thoughts for the week, and some preliminary actions toward problem resolution. This is a good time to show the contract. The worker merely hands the copy to the client explaining that this is a letter spelling out the what is to come if they decide to continue working together. The worker simply asks the client to read it carefully before the next session.

When that time comes, the worker begins the second session by asking if the client has read the contract. Whether or not the answer is yes, the worker spends a few minutes going over its most important points with the client. This is important to make sure every element is understood. Once the worker is sure the client understands, the goals of the helping relationship are discussed. Together the worker and client spend part of the session deciding on these goals and in stating them in specific and do-able terms. Then the worker and client can write these goals on the contract in the space provided.

The worker and client each have identical copies of the contract and the explicated goals, both of which are signed by both participants. During the ongoing therapeutic work the goals can be period-ically reviewed. So, too, can any other of the contract's elements. This helps define, focus, and minimize misunderstandings.

CONCLUSION

Studies show that the written contract is a useful and effective tool in the worker-client intervention process (Seabury, 1987). When constructed systematically and implemented properly, a con-tract can minimize misunderstandings and risks of malpractice and peer review. Moreover, it can provide the worker and client with greater focus toward goal achievement.

Obviously a written contract is not a panacea to eliminate all the potential difficulties confronting social workers in direct practice. Even when written contracts are used, malpractice suits will some-times be instigated, peer review committees will be formed, and clients will be confused or disappointed about their goals and pro-gression. Nevertheless, the likelihood of problems for the worker will be significantly reduced with written contracts. And most im-portant of all, clients will be more efficiently and effectively served.

Chapter 7

Legal and Professional Credentials

The legal regulation of social work practice is a relatively recent phenomenon. Licensing laws have been passed in the majority of states in only the past 20 years. Now all states legally regulate social work practice through licenses, certification, or registration. However, there is little uniformity between the states as to these regulations. Laws differ dramatically as to qualifications, enforcement, and strength. Because these differences are often confusing to social workers as well as to consumers, the purpose of this chapter is to review the licensing process, discuss the functions of licenses, and consider their virtues and deficiencies.

THE PURPOSE OF LEGAL REGULATION

The purpose of legal regulation of social work practice and professional certification is to provide the public with a priori evidence that specified standards have been met. When consumers seek providers of services, they are entitled to know what the provider's background and current capabilities are. Usually consumers have no other way of knowing whether the potential provider is competent or not. Obviously, clients would find it inconvenient, costly, and emotionally distracting to go from one provider to another in the hope of finding out.

The license or professional certificate gives the consumer some important information about the holder of that document. With the backing of state law, the license tells the consumer that the worker has achieved certain levels of education, experience, and abilities. Of course, this information does not constitute proof that the worker is currently competent, but it does give the consumer some assurances that the worker has fulfilled the licensing criteria.

Legal regulation and professional certification is important for social workers to establish credibility with clients, colleagues, law courts, legislators, and the public at large. Without documentation of this type, the social worker is not usually eligible for third-party payments and is limited as to the reimbursement that can be obtained from agencies or private clients. However, because there are so many variations in legal regulation and professional certification, the worker faces a challenge in merely trying to understand the situation.

LICENSING AND OTHER CREDENTIALS

Social workers are affected by many types of licenses, professional certificates, and other forms of quality control. These include the workers' degrees from accredited professional schools, certificates of post-graduate education, and the accumulation of continuing education credits, all accompanied by various diplomas usually hung on office walls. Also included are memberships in relevant professional organizations which specify and enforce the requirements for membership and monitor compliance with the codes of ethics.

Professional associations also sponsor special certification for some of their members who meet additional criteria. The Academy of Certified Social Workers, for example, is open only to more experienced members of the National Association of Social Workers, and a few others who have maintained specified continuing education requirements. Certificates of this type typically tell the consumer that the worker has achieved some explicated indicator of expertise.

These credentials may have some merit, but they have little authority in the law and any deviations from them are dealt with "in-house." Thus, if a social worker violates some professional standard, the police or prosecutor is not called. The professional association itself investigates and decides on the appropriate sanction, primarily through a professional Committee on Inquiry, peer review association, or similar group. These will be discussed in Chapter 8.

TYPES OF LEGAL REGULATION

When professional practice occurs under legal auspices, it is the state, not the profession, that ultimately has the right and obligation to protect the public. Credentials that have the authority of law behind them include registration and certification, as well as licensure. The state licensing (or equivalent) boards regulate these laws, set standards, investigate alleged deviations from those standards, and facilitate punishment for those considered deserving of it.

Of the three forms of legal regulation, registration is the weakest and licensing is the strongest (Hardcastle, 1990). In registration, the weakest form of legal regulation, the state merely lists people who identify themselves as social workers, and may punish those who falsely claim to be in the registry. However, the state has no authority to punish those who call themselves social workers, as long as they do not claim to be registered. In certification, the state awards certificates to social workers who apply and document that they have achieved certain levels and types of skill and education. However, the state does not punish anyone unless that person claims to be certified by the state.

Licensing is the strongest form of legal regulation because it explicates education, knowledge, and skill requirements, and uses the state's regulatory powers to ensure that the worker's behavior complies with the required standards. The relevant licensing law indicates the right of the state to protect the public through applying sanctions to any licensee who violates the standards. Thus, the consumer of the social work service as well as the third party which pays for it have some assurance that the worker is meeting the specified standards. The profession itself is also protected from incompetent workers who, if left unregulated, would give the profession a poor image.

STRUCTURE OF LICENSING BOARDS

The social work licensing system is usually operated in a fashion similar to the licensing for the other professions (Flynn, 1987). In those states (and other jurisdictions where licensure exists, such as Washington, D.C., Puerto Rico, and Guam), it is administered by a board of examiners or supervisors. This board may be exclusively for social work licensure, or in some cases it is part of a board which administers licensure for many professional groups.

The statute which establishes this board is passed by the state legislature and signed by the governor, and usually includes provisions for the management, financing, and regulation of the system. Sometimes these laws specify the qualifications of the licensee, as well as continuing standards and procedures for enforcement; other laws indicate that such elements will be determined by the board or its designees.

The boards of social work examiners may or may not be exclusively social workers. Since the members are appointed by the governor or other executive, they may be political allies, bureaucrats, or members of related professions, as well as social workers. Usually the governor follows some or all of the appointment recommendations of the state social work associations, especially those which spearheaded the legislation that created the law. In most states the board members serve for a specified length of time, after which the governor replaces or reappoints them.

Nearly all the state licensure boards now belong to the American Association of State Social Work Boards (AASSWB), headquartered in Virginia. This organization facilitates communication between the various boards, and advises the boards about such matters as developing competency tests, continuing education requirements, recertification policies, and reciprocity.

FUNCTIONS OF THE LICENSING BOARD

Once a state board is established it determines, within the specifications of the licensure law, how workers will become licensed. They establish the ground rules, with proper input from professional associations, concerned individual social workers, client consumer groups, third-party organizations, and government and legal authorities. The ground rules will indicate qualifications for licensure, such as level of education, experience, specialty, and proof of competence.

Proof of competence is supposedly established through systematic licensing examinations and documentation of continuing education requirements. In the jurisdictions where formal examinations are required, the board develops the exams and procedures for taking them. Frequently it does this by hiring consultants who specialize in professional testing development. The tests themselves are created by panels of social workers who design questions, answers, and appropriate "distractors" (the term applied to the incorrect multiple-choice test answers.) Before use, the exams are carefully pretested; experienced and knowledgeable social work volunteers take the exams and the results are analyzed. Test items whose results are inconsistent with the rest of the exam are discarded.

In the actual examinations given to license applicants, test designers incorporate several prototype test items which look identical to the other test items, but which are not counted in the final results. These prototype items are then analyzed as to consistency with the rest of the exam, and if they prove to be valid may be included in subsequent editions of the test.

The board also maintains records of the status of each licensed social worker, informs licensees and consumers about the standards for licensure, and, where applicable, maintains records about continuing education. The board and the licensure procedure is financed entirely from annual fees which licensed workers pay to be eligible for licensure.

COMPARING CREDENTIALS IN OTHER PROFESSIONS

Social work, compared to most of the other health and mental health professions, has lagged behind. The other professions — especially psychiatry, psychology, and nursing — have stronger licensing laws in every state. Moreover, their standards and requirements for licensure are more consistent from state to state than is the case with social work. Every state requires the licensed members of these professions to meet educational and experience criteria and pass examinations. They require their licensed members to demonstrate proof of continuing competency by taking a specified number of approved training hours and by being required to take periodic continuing education tests. As a result, the public is fairly well protected against incompetent or malevolent practitioners, and their respective professions are able to weed out members who fail to meet standards. As a further result, the public and the established third-party financing organizations seek the services of these professionals with little reservation.

The legal regulation of social work does not compare favorably with that of the other disciplines. The various states that license social workers have different requirements. In some states, no one has to take examinations to become licensed. In other states, only younger workers need to take the examinations. Some states require that their licensed social workers submit periodic proof that they have taken continuing education credits; others use the "honor system" if they have any continuing education requirements at all.

Professional regulation of social workers' practices also compares unfavorably with that of the other disciplines. Social workers belong to many different professional organizations, each of which maintains its own code of ethics, educational requirements, continuing competency standards, and requirements for admission-expulsion. These organizations include the National Association of Social Workers, the National Federation of Societies for Clinical Social Work, the International Federation of Social Workers, the National Association of Black Social Workers, the National Academy of Practice in Social Work, the National Registry of Health Care Providers in Clinical Social Work, and many others.

Partly under the sponsorship of some of these associations, other organizations have been created to define, set standards for, and monitor social work practice and then offer credentials. These organizations include the Academy of Certified Social Workers, the American Board of Examiners in Clinical Social Work, and various others certification authorities, each with distinct regulations and requirements. Some of these organizations are overtly competitive and hostile toward one another. Two organizations, the National Association of Social Workers and the American Board of Examiners in Social Work, have initiated litigation against one another.

The issue they have disputed is ostensibly about broken agreements; however, most objective observers see it as a dispute over power and turf.

DEVELOPMENT OF CREDENTIALING PROBLEMS

How is it that the social work profession has not kept pace with other professions in its credentialing and licensing procedures? The answer can be understood better by reviewing the history of social work credentialing.

When social work emerged as an identifiable occupation in the 1890s and as a profession in the 1920s, its primary practice was within social agencies. Nearly all workers were employees of government or private social agencies. Clients sought services from the agency/employer rather than the worker. The agencies were accountable for any problems so they exercised great care in their hiring and supervising of social work employees.

The social work establishment did not perceive any particular need for legal regulation because the public was well protected through the agency model, perhaps better than any of the other professions. Clients paid the agency for services, and the fees were subsidized through contributions and public fund raising efforts. Thus, there were no third-party financing organizations involved to help motivate the profession to achieve greater accountability standards.

Because social agency employment was predominant, and still is by far the primary employer of social workers, most people saw little need for additional regulation. It was believed that the supervisors could do everything needed. It seemed to most social workers that licensing was something only for private social work practitioners, a small proportion of the membership. And most social workers thought private practice was anathema to the goals and values of the profession (Barker, 1991b).

Nevertheless, some social workers and others recognized the need for regulation outside social agencies. In 1917 social workers themselves developed an employment registry, indicating the qualifications of those who could be listed. This grouping eventually formed the American Association of Social Workers, which in 1955 merged with other groups to become the National Association of Social Workers. NASW and its state chapters made few attempts and had little success in getting states to pass social work licensing laws until the late 1960s.

In lieu of this, in 1962 NASW developed a certificate program, restricted to experienced professional social workers, known as the Academy of Certified Social Workers. Requirements for ACSW eligibility, not high to begin with, have been lowered since inception to permit more social workers to be admitted.

The other social work organizations, unhappy with NASW's perceived lack of enthusiasm for nonclinical practice and licensing statutes, started forming in the 1970s. Through the efforts of these groups, and the redoubled efforts of NASW in response, various states began passing licensing laws. However, because of the different types of organizations and different degrees of enthusiasm involved, the licensing laws that were passed varied widely.

CONSEQUENCES OF THE PROBLEM

To many social workers, legal regulation of practice is not a serious issue. What difference does it make, they wonder, whether social work is regulated by licensing or by agency administrators and supervisors? The public will be protected just as much in the one system as in the other. And maybe the public is protected more through individualized agency supervision than it could ever be through impersonal licensing exams.

The fact is, however, that it is a serious issue. Rigorous, standardized licensing regulations are essential to the profession and all its practitioners, including those who continue to work in agencies. Social work now must compete with other professions that have more stringent credentials. These professions, especially nursing and psychology, are now performing many of the functions that were once the recognized province of social work.

Payment for social work services, in agencies as well as private practice, is now largely underwritten by insurance companies and other third-party payers, who increasingly demand legal regulation. They have excluded social work from reimbursement in many localities where licensing was nonexistent, weak, or inconsistent. The consumer and the worker both are likely to be confused about the hodge-podge of standards and rules for workers. The image of the profession would be hard pressed to improve in the face of such obstacles.

RESISTANCE TO SOCIAL WORK LICENSURE

On the face of it licensing seems to be good for all concerned, including the public at large, the social worker, the agency employer, the private practitioner, the insurance company, the profession, and especially the consumer. Nevertheless, there has been considerable active resistance against the development of social work licensing laws. This is why it has taken more than 30 years to get licensure of social work passed in all the states.

Pressures against licensure continues. Under sunset legislation, many of the states with such laws periodically reevaluate whether or not to retain social work licensure. Legislators in some states have been working to eliminate existing social work licensure laws or to incorporate them with licenses for other professions such as marital and family therapists, pastoral counselors, and similar groups.

The resistance to social work licensure comes from many sources, including some competing professions, third-party organizations, legislators, and even social workers themselves. Some professional groups, such as psychology, have testified against licensing social workers in some states; they argue that some of the activities specified in the proposed legislation should be theirs exclusively. They want to restrict competition, so they pressure legislators to vote against stronger social work licensure.

Some financial planners and budget analysts with government and third-party organizations have also argued against social work licensure. They claim that social work licensure opens the door to many more service providers who would make claims for providing health care services and driving up costs. Other third-party representatives have argued that the opposite is true. They point out that social workers' fees are somewhat lower than those of other professions so the costs would more likely be driven lower rather than raised. However, there is no reliable evidence yet available that proves third-party outlays are higher or lower when social workers become licensed.

Resistance has also come from economic and political leaders who have argued to eliminate or reduce all professional licensure. These people gained force during the years of the Reagan Administration. They claimed that licensing professionals was a way to restrict supply of service providers. Market forces, they feel, would govern a profession more efficiently than would a legislatively imposed scheme.

OBJECTIONS TO SOCIAL WORK LICENSURE

Some social workers themselves have fought against licensure. They have been indifferent or antipathetic toward licensing laws because they want to maintain the status quo or feel that licensure will be disadvantageous to some groups within the profession (Iverson, 1987). They indicate that social work does not need to be licensed if all its activity occurs within the auspices of a publicly regulated agency. In this sense, some of their objections are actually against private practice. Some agency supervisors and administrators have resisted licensure possibly because they want to maintain more of their power over the worker by providing the only regulation and accountability that would otherwise exist.

A recurring obstacle to licensure has been in identifying what social workers do that is exclusive. Licenses are issued to lawyers, physicians, and even morticians because they are the only ones permitted to do what they do. Social work has had a difficult time making this claim of an exclusive function (Middleman, 1984). Until the profession satisfactorily resolves this issue, it will continue to be difficult to gain acceptable licensure statutes.

Another obstacle from within social work has to do with the difficulty of finding suitable measures of competence. To have a license, the licensing authority needs to be able to distinguish between those social workers who can do the job and those who cannot. The tests of competence have been attacked by various social workers (Johnson and Huff, 1987). They have said such tests do not accurately measure social work competence, that they are culturally biased, that they are too heavily weighted toward clinical knowledge, are too heavily weighted toward psychoanalytic theory, or that the conditions in which they are given are so poor that they prove nothing (Borenzweig, 1977).

Because of so much widespread dissatisfaction, those fighting against licensing statutes have been easily able to find opponents who have been aggrieved by the process. However, resistance due to these problems are diminishing as the examinations and conditions in which they are administered are improving (Dolan, 1988).

Finally, some resistance to licensure comes from social workers who themselves feel threatened or inconvenienced by the imposition of new requirements. Many of these people see the need for licensure, but do not want its requirements to apply to them. They seemingly prefer weak or nonexistent regulations for all colleagues if it means they do not have to risk failure themselves.

DEFICIENCIES IN CURRENT LICENSING LAWS

Whether the resistance to licensure from within and without grows or declines, it is clear that licensure is here to stay. If for no other reasons, competition for clients and retaining eligibility for third-party payments will make licensing a necessity. But the value of the license will be vitiated as long as its most glaring problems persist. The four most serious problems are: (1) the conflict between social work organizations about the operation of licensure laws; (2) the lack of standardization in qualifications for social work credentialing; (3) the grandparenting rules in credentialing; and (4) inadequate continuing education requirements and enforcement procedures.

The first difficulty, that of internal conflicts between social work organizations, is the most serious and the heart of the other problems. So many social workers are dissatisfied with existing licensing laws, credentialing bodies, and the types of standards, that they form their own groups. They hope to remedy the situation by developing new criteria and standards for licensure and then attracting workers to their credentialing authority. This leads to rivalry between social work groups and confusion for everyone else.

The recent litigation between the new American Board of Examiners in Clinical Social Work (ABE) and the National Association of Social Workers is only one example. Both groups are competing to be the major professional credentialing authority for social workers by creating new certificate programs. Unfortunately, they have devoted many of their finite resources to legally combatting the rival group than to improve the credentialing situation.

Competing groups is one reason for the second credentialing deficiency, that of the wide disparity of standards for social work credentials. Each state has unique criteria for social work credentials. It makes a great difference to the worker, the consumer, the third party, and the public whether the work goes on in one jurisdiction or another. Workers must decide in which state to seek employment, depending on the qualifications they have to offer.

The need for uniform or more similar standards should be the next goal of the profession, now that legal regulation has been achieved everywhere. When the standards are closer to uniformity and consistency, it will be possible to grant reciprocity for workers practicing across state lines.

THE GRANDPARENT RULE

The third deficiency in social work credentialing is that of grandparenting. This refers to the practice of exempting experienced social workers from qualifying examinations and other eligibility requirements that apply to newer workers. In nearly every legal jurisdiction and professional credentialing body, some form of grandparent exclusion exists. The rationale is that the veteran social worker is already so experienced that he or she should not have to prove merit through the examination.

The stated rationale is dubious. Experience does not guarantee that the worker has kept current. Furthermore, many older workers with experience in another social work specialty are granted this waiver even though they have little experience in the work for which they now want to be licensed. If the purpose of legal and professional regulation is to protect the consumer then grandparenting undercuts the purpose.

Experienced workers have argued other reasons for being waived: they claim that the exams are poorly administered, culturally biased, irrelevant to current social work practice, and generally not good indicators of competence. If this is so, then it is not any more appropriate to expect it of younger workers. Moreover, the examinations and procedures are improving significantly and these complaints are rarely heard anymore. Nevertheless, the demand for grandparenting continues.

Clearly the grandparenting waiver is not granted because of rationality or fairness. It is granted because the experienced social workers have the power and they do not want to run the risk of embarrassment in taking the tests. They want to share in the benefits of the credentials, that is third-party recognition, increased prestige, and protection of the public, but they are less enthused about the effort to make credentialing work.

CONTINUING EDUCATION REQUIREMENTS

Similar to the grandparenting problem is that of continuing education. Inadequate requirements and enforcement procedures prevail. Professional knowledge is not static and must be continually upgraded and developed for it to be valid. Studies show that half the knowledge possessed by a professional becomes outdated and must be replaced every few years (Robinowitz and Greenblatt, 1980; Dubin, 1981). Thus, for social workers to remain competent, some form of continuing education is a necessity. If this competence is to be certified by some legal or professional body, some form of documentation or proof is in order (Seelig, 1990).

Most professions document the continuing competence of their members by periodic reexaminations and by requiring specified units of continuing education within accredited schools or professional meetings. For example, lawyers in most states are required to take 15 hours of certified courses per year or 45 hours over any running three year period. Some physician specialties require members to earn 45 units per year. Other professions also require proof of continuing education. In some states, the licensed professional must file an annual affidavit with the board. In others, attendees must sign in for each continuing education session. The provider then certifies the names to the professional association. Some professional groups use both systems.

For the most part, social work has not yet achieved this standard.

Many social work regulatory boards have no specific requirements about continuing education. Others indicate that continuing education is needed but do not require proof of its acquisition. Theoretically, the worker keeps track of the number of educational hours logged, and presents the number to any board that asks. Rarely do they ask.

Related to continuing education is the issue of periodic reexamination. Few jurisdictions or professional organizations presently require social workers to be examined in order to retain their licenses or certificates. Even if the worker accumulated continuing education credits, it is no assurance that the information has been relevant or retained. Nearly all the other professions, occupational groups, and even state drivers' license boards, require this. But for now it seems highly unlikely that a profession that excuses its older workers from licensing examinations would require them to take periodic reexaminations. Clients can only hope that the experienced social workers they have dealt with are personally conscientious enough to remain up to date of their own volitions.

Chapter 8

Adjudication Through Professional Review

Malpractice suits, criminal cases, and licensure hearings are not always the most appropriate mechanisms for protecting clients and policing a profession. The following two cases illustrate:

A social worker recently treated a couple for marital problems. The short-term treatment was successful. Both the husband and wife were pleased with the worker's efforts. Eventually the couple submitted a claim to their health insurance company, despite the company's explicit disclaimer indicating it does not reimburse for the treatment of marital problems. Knowing this, but recognizing that the couple could not afford the service without insurance reimbursement, the worker submitted an insurance claim nonetheless. With the clients' concurrence, the worker identified the wife as the patient and stated that all the therapy sessions were for her problem of "dysthymic disorder" (depression). The company did reimburse for treatment of this condition.

The worker rationalized that the wife actually was depressed because of her marriage, and that the best treatment for the depression was to resolve marital problems. Accordingly, the husband was seen alone during several sessions, as was the wife. When the insurance company learned that it was being charged for services rendered not to the identified client, but to the client's husband, it acted against the worker. The insurance company decided to exclude the social worker from all future reimbursements.

In another case, a private practice social worker decided to stop treating a client after six months. The client was diagnosed with anxiety problems and sexual dysfunction. As treatment progressed, with good results, the client began falling behind on payments and seemed indifferent to the worker's insistence on catching up. Eventually the worker terminated sessions. The termination process included an appropriate referral to a community mental health center which would be affordable to the client. Nevertheless, the client decided to take action against the worker for the ethical violation of premature termination of services.

THE NEED FOR ALTERNATIVES TO COURTS OF LAW

In both these cases, and thousands of others, the most appropriate forum for adjudication may not be courts of law. In the first case, the insurance company could hardly charge malpractice, and would probably be loathe to attempt initiation of costly criminal charges of embezzlement. In the second case, the aggrieved client would have a difficult time retaining a lawyer to take such a case to the malpractice court. Moreover, the state licensing board would not likely force the worker to continue seeing the client. Where could the client or the worker get a fair hearing or the third party go to get a fair and forceful decision?

An alternative forum for adjudicating differences and policing professional practice is in order, and in fact exists for all professionals. Social work practice is scrutinized by the worker's professional association, the government professional review organization in the relevant jurisdiction, the peer review committee of third-party organizations, the worker's employer/agency, and the review committee of the state licensing board.

Professional associations, employers, and third parties seek to control the professional's work ultimately for their own protection and self-interest. Each of these entities has its own procedures to determine whether or not the worker has engaged in wrongdoing and for punishing those who do. If they did not have such mechanisms, it would be necessary for grievances to be adjudicated by the public legal system. This would be costly and highly time consuming. Airing the profession's "dirty linen" in public would also be painful for all concerned.

More importantly, if all grievances against professionals had to be adjudicated in the public courts of law or licensing boards, it would also diminish the profession's ability to maintain its own standards. Every profession requires its members to perform their duties within the bounds of explicit standards. The professions claim they do so to provide additional protection to society and their clientele from the possible wrongdoing of their members; but they also do so to maintain public credibility and esteem. Organizations that employ professionals, such as hospitals and social service agencies, have the same concerns. If a high percentage of employer's workers or a profession's members were publicly exposed as incompetent or malevolent, there would be a precipitous decline in the organization's or profession's prestige.

Third parties or host organizations which employ professionals have a strong interest in assuring that their employees are doing their jobs properly. Otherwise they could be paying for services that are not needed or not provided; or they could be seen by the public as sponsoring activities that are harmful to clients. This could jeopardize the very existence of the operation. Thus, the third party or host organizations, usually in a contractual relationship with the professional, specifies the expectations that the professional must meet; and they can also impose punishments or sanctions according to contracted procedures.

For the most part the profession, the employer, and the third party's interests are protected by the worker's own sense of responsibility, personal ethical standards, and other internal controls. These standards are mostly developed through the worker's formal education and professional socialization experiences. Clearly the internal controls are more important to workers' meeting professional standards than any coercion or external threats could ever be (Siporin, 1982).

If, on the other hand, the professional person has a grievance against a client, there is no alternative but the legal justice system (Miller and Maier, 1990). Such grievances are rare and have mostly been in the realm of fee disputes and, to a lesser extent, to client physical abuse of the worker. So far, society and the legal system have not appeared to be very favorably disposed toward protecting or compensating workers who have been injured by clients (Schultz, 1989; Miller et al., 1990).

PHILOSOPHIES OF REVIEWING ORGANIZATIONS

The professional associations that have peer review mechanisms for social workers are the National Association of Social Workers (NASW), the American Board of Examiners in Clinical Social Work (ABE), and the National Federation of Societies for Clinical Social Work (NFSCSW). Other professional associations that exist for specific social work populations, such as the National Association of Black Social Workers and the Association of Native American Social Workers, have been working toward developing peer review mechanisms. Peer review mechanisms are also sponsored by professional associations whose memberships come from many disciplines including social work. These include the American Association for Marriage and Family Therapy (AAMFT) and the American Association of Sex Educators, Counselors and Therapists (AASECT).

Government organizations that sponsor professional review procedures include the congressionally mandated Peer Review Organizations (also known as Professional Standards Review Organizations, or PSROs, and as Professional Review Organizations). The federal government also sponsors third-party funding organizations such as the CHAMPUS health insurance program for military dependents and retired military personnel.

Each system has its own goals and philosophy of review, which results in their own procedures for adjudication. The professional associations focus on behaviors that deviate from their codes of ethics and result in harm to clients. State licensing committees are oriented to whether any laws have been broken by the professional who holds the state license. The government organizations and third-party insurance companies focus on cost containment issues and whether the professional is charging fees appropriately.

Those who serve on review committees are generally professional colleagues. Often their expertise is in the same realm as the person whose work is being reviewed. Usually the committee members are volunteers who serve, not on a case by case ad hoc basis, but for all the cases that come up during a specified term. Usually the members of such panels are experienced, well-established professionals in their own right whose goals are to help preserve the integrity of the profession and protect clients from those who might lack professional integrity. The professionals who serve recognize that the legal risks of participating in peer review are not as great as some might fear (Qualliotine, 1991).

TYPES OF SANCTIONS

Because professional associations or third parties have no legal authority over service providers and members of the profession, the punishments or sanctions imposed seem generally less severe. Unlike the legal system, which can incarcerate the professional or require payment of damages, the greatest punishment that these organizations can impose is expulsion and/or financial penalties.

The most severe sanction usually taken by a third-party organization is to disqualify the worker from further eligibility to receive funds for services. In some communities and states, the third-party organization does so by removing the professional's name from its list of preferred providers. Other sanctions include financial penalties. A third party can require the professional or the professional's employer/agency to repay monies that it considers were improperly received. Usually the third-party organization accomplishes return of fees, not by requiring direct repayments, but by deducting the amount from future payments.

Employers of social workers exercise their sanctions primarily through personnel actions. They can, of course, fire their workers, give them less desirable assignments, or withhold promotions and pay raises.

The most severe sanction imposed by a professional association is expulsion. Other punishments may include suspension of membership until certain requirements are met, continued membership on some probationary status, and continued membership while fulfilling requirements made by the association. Some professional associations publicize the wrongdoing of the member by specifying in their newsletters and journals the name of the member and the particular part of the ethics code that has been violated. By itself, expulsion from the professional association may not seem to a social worker to be a severe penalty; a social worker usually might still practice without the professional association's blessing. However, the expelled individual also loses credibility, clientele, and peer group association. This person is also more vulnerable to the far more compelling punishment, that of losing the legal right to practice in the jurisdiction through loss of license. In such a case, the professional cannot depend on the association or its members to offer much assistance when the licensing authority challenges the person's continued right to practice.

Ultimately, sanctions made by professional associations and third parties are highly undesirable. Not only do they involve loss of face and peer contact but economic loss as well. The resulting diminished professional credibility can translate into economic losses that far exceed the losses faced by malpractice litigation.

THIRD-PARTY REVIEW PROCEDURES

The third-party review organizations and the federally mandated professional review organizations do not wait for complaints to be filed against professionals. They monitor the records of those cases they help to finance. The cases to be reviewed are often selected at random from the forms that are submitted for reimbursement, or from hospital or agency charts. The work of some professionals or service providing agencies is scrutinized more intensely if they have had previous problems.

The panel of reviewers, usually paid physicians and other professionals, determine if the work done is justified and appropriate for the stated diagnosis. For example, if a worker submits a claim for three years of intense psychotherapy for a client with agoraphobia, the panel would probably require further justification from the worker, because this disorder is usually treated successfully with short-term therapy approaches. When disparities between the diagnosis and the expected treatment are identified, the panel notifies the provider of the inquiry and asks for specific information.

The panel may accept the information provided and authorize payment. Or it may make an adjustment and authorize partial payment only. Or it may reject the claim outright, in which case the payment is withheld. Typically the panel or the third-party organization does not demand a repayment from the service provider, but deducts sums from future claims. On those rare occasions when the panel suspects fraud or unethical conduct based on the available records, the panel may notify the legal and professional authorities.

The panelists who participate in these reviews are employed by the government or the third party. In the case of social workers being reviewed, the panelists have not always been colleagues. Sometimes psychiatrists and other physicians have evaluated the professional practice of social workers. Rarely do social workers evaluate psychiatrists.

Government scrutiny of professional practice has been reduced significantly in the past decade. The government organizations which were established for this purpose came into being in 1972 and were known as Professional Standards Review Organizations (PSROs). At that time Congress enacted amendments to the Social Security Act (PL 92-603) to make sure that taxpayers' money was being well-spent on health care, especially Medicare and Medicaid. PSROs were revised and reduced considerably with 1982 amendments to the law (Marcus, 1987).

THE NASW ADJUDICATION PROCEDURE

The NASW procedure for professional review of social worker conduct is the oldest and most tested procedure, having become the model upon which most other peer review processes are based. Even most state licensing boards have modeled their adjudication procedures after NASW. Thus, NASW procedures are a paradigm one might examine in order to understand any of the other professional review procedures to which one might be subjected.

The adjudication process applies to two broad categories of cases, allegations of ethical malfeasance by an individual social worker who belongs to NASW, and violations of personnel standards alleged against agencies which employ social workers (Osman and Shueman, 1988).

The primary mechanism for implementing the adjudication procedure is through the local NASW chapters Committees on Inquiry (COIs), and the NASW National Committee on Inquiry (NCOI). The NCOI provides each COI with written guidelines, provides advice, and monitors the COI to assure compliance. The local NASW chapter appoints members to staff the COI. The COI members decide whether a given case meets the criteria for review. After a case has been reviewed, the COI reports its findings and recommendations to the chapter.

Cases come to the attention of the COI when a client or worker calls the NASW chapter to lodge the complaint. The adjudication guidelines specify that the case will not be considered for review unless the complaint is made within 60 days after the client or worker comes to believe that a wrong has been committed. However, because complainants often need more time to recover or summon the nerve to formally make the allegation, this time limit is often waived (Berliner, 1989).

Usually the complainant calls the local NASW chapter office to make the allegation. The office then provides information about how to file a formal declaration. The complainant must allege exactly which principle of the Code of Ethics has been violated in order for the case to be accepted. Chapter staff also help the complainant throughout the process to obtain the proper information, identify proper jurisdiction, and to frame the allegation in a reviewable way. Staff review the written declaration to determine if it is properly and completely filled out. The COI is then convened to determine if the case should be accepted. If it is not, the complainant may appeal the decision to the national COI.

When a case is accepted, the COI notifies both the complainant and respondent about the time, place, circumstances, and participants. Either party may challenge the participation of any member of the review panel "who they believe to be prejudiced with respect to the matter to be adjudicated. Such a challenge, stating reasons, shall be submitted in writing to the chairman of the inquiry committee who will inform the member who challenged and provide an opportunity for voluntary disqualification" (NASW, 1980, p. 6).

At the hearing, either party may bring an NASW member for assistance in presenting the case. They have the right to be present when witnesses are called by the panel and to ask questions of those witnesses. While they are entitled to seek the assistance of counsel or others in the preparation of their cases, they may not bring lawyers to the hearing.

After the formal hearing, the panel has 45 days in which to report its recommendations. If the conclusion sustains the allegations by the complainant, the statement specifies which element of the Code has been violated. The statements also recommend the type of punishments to be levied. The recommendation is reviewed by the full chapter COI and the chapter board members. The chapter executive officers may not reverse COI decisions. However, they may modify (but not increase) the recommended punishments.

The final report is sent by certified mail to the NCOI and to both parties in the dispute. Either party may appeal the decision within the following 30 days. The other party is then notified about the appeal and has the right to rebut the appeal within 30 days. The NCOI then reviews the written documents relative to the appeal, but does not permit the parties to make personal appearances in the review. However, either party may make a further appeal to the NASW board of directors if dissatisfied with the rulings of the NCOI.

OUTCOMES OF NASW REVIEWS

When the complainant's allegations are sustained through this process, the punishments are imposed by the National Association of Social Workers. The most common sanctions are private censure or supervision of the worker's practice for a specified time. Only the national Committee on Inquiry or the NASW Board may suspend or expel the respondent from continued membership. The worker may appeal to NCOI or to the NASW Board of Directors.

The types of cases that are heard by COIs vary. The most common complaints include: sexual misconduct; breach of confidentiality; fee splitting; soliciting the clients of other workers; overall professional misconduct; failing to adhere to ethical responsibilities to colleagues; and failing to fulfill ethical responsibilities to organizations, the social work profession, or society.

About 10 percent of the cases brought to COIs are withdrawn before any hearing commences. Individuals withdraw their complaints for reasons such as fear of being further traumatized, deciding to pursue legal action instead, or to try to resolve their differences with the worker independently of any formal adjudication process.

Another 10 percent of all complaints do not receive formal hearings because of decisions by the Committee on Inquiry not to look into the matter. COIs decide this for several reasons. Some complaints are made against workers who are not NASW members and therefore outside the COI jurisdiction. Other complaints do not involve violations of ethical standards so the issue to be adjudicated is outside the realm of the COI. Another reason is that the complaint has not been issued within the 60 day "statute of limitations" which the NASW guidelines specify as necessary.

The cases that are fully adjudicated by the COI and NCOI usually take several months and sometimes years to resolve. NASW reports (1980) that one-third took at least nine months and 20 percent took more than a year. Observance of careful procedures and multi-tiered review processes account for much of the delay. But COI and NCOI adjudication is not a screen behind which the profession hides. COIs have determined in 41 percent of the cases that some violation of ethical standards did indeed take place.

CRITIQUE OF NASW ADJUDICATION PROCEDURES

Some social workers, especially those who have been subjected to NASW adjudication, have found fault with the NASW review procedures. Many believe that the process takes too long, primarily because the volunteers who serve on COI panels are busy with their own employment and are not available to serve on such panels as speedily as might be desired. Berliner (1989) suggests that this problem could be minimized through the greater utilization of retired or semi-retired colleagues to serve on such panels.

NASW has been criticized for its policy of excluding legal counsel at hearings. Lawyers are permitted, even required, at most civil and criminal court proceedings, and are considered essential in protecting the rights of the relevant parties. NASW points out that the Supreme Court has ruled that participation of a lawyer is not an element of due process unless imprisonment may be a result. It contends that law training is not universally required for the proper decision of professional questions. NASW further states that legal representation of one party at grievance and adjudication proceedings may be "counterproductive and would place the parties on an unequal footing" (NASW Chapter Guide, 1980, p. 6).

Zastrow, in an important critique of these procedures (1991), is concerned about the lack of opportunity to interview members of the hearing panel in advance to determine whether bias exists. In the legal justice system, opposing lawyers have the chance to interview and challenge prospective jurors, and sometimes to even move for a change of judges. But the parties in reviews do not have the right to challenge panel members, even for cause.

Zastrow also examines four other potential procedural defects: (1) the opportunity for the parties involved to be present during appeals is lacking; (2) the worker may be subject to "double jeopardy" in that the grievance may be heard by the panel after other authorities (licensing boards, ethics boards of other professional associations, law courts) may have already heard the case and ruled in favor of the worker; (3) verbatim transcripts are not taken during hearings and thus are not available for internal review or for the appeal process; and (4) the hearing panels sometimes bend their own rules rather than adhere to rigid procedures as is the case in legal hearings.

OTHER ADJUDICATION PROCEDURES

Despite potential problems, the NASW adjudication procedure is more carefully delineated and implemented than most of the alternatives, including the government, Professional Review Organizations, third-party systems, and even many state licensing boards (Hardcastle, 1990). Those which do specify the conduct expected of licensed workers tend to base the standard on the NASW delineated standards.

In a few of the states that have rigorous social work licensing laws, the system closely approximates the NASW model. When an individual alleges that a licensed worker has violated the standards of professional practice, these social work licensing boards may appoint panels of colleagues to review the matter. Usually these boards seek the services of NASW or another relevant professional association in the jurisdiction; sometimes the panel for professional review and licensing review are synonymous. Licensing boards are more likely than NASW to permit the participation of lawyers and to require written transcripts of testimony if the case might lead to expulsion, probation, or publicity.

In the professional review systems of government or third-party organizations, such as PROs and PSROs, the disputes are often not between worker and client, but between worker/client and the third party. The review panel often audits the worker's records without the worker's knowledge to ascertain if the treatment was in accordance with the stated diagnosis, and if that treatment could have been done more efficiently.

Only after the review panel determines that some discrepancy exists is the worker then likely to invoke rights to a defense. Defense occurs first by written and oral responses to questions from the panel, usually requesting justifications for the procedures taken. The panel may, but rarely does, contact the client for verification of the stated treatments. The worker may dispute the decisions the review panel makes, but because the penalty is mostly about money received for past services rendered, most workers do not pursue the matter. However, they may retain counsel, initiating actions against the review panel. These contentions may then be heard by the panel itself or in a public court of law.

THE INEVITABILITY OF PEER REVIEW

In the modern era, a professional person cannot avoid being scrutinized and subjected to peer reviews of some sort. Peer review will certainly occur when professional misconduct is credibly alleged, and will also occur in random audits and examinations of the professional's records. Thus, a professional who asks, "How can I avoid peer reviews?" is asking the wrong question. The right question is, "How can I avoid sanctions?"

Obviously, sanctions are less likely to be imposed on the worker who adheres to the ethics and standards of the profession and fulfills the obligations required by third parties. However, the worker must be well-versed in what these ethics, standards, and obligations are. Studies have shown that many workers are woefully underinformed about professional standards (Berliner, 1989).

Even when the worker is knowledgeable about the standards and has an avowed intention to meet them, problems can arise. As we have seen in previous chapters, the standards are sometimes contradictory, unclear, and impossible to meet. At times standards are perceived as being unfair to the worker. But professional review will be better for most workers than the public courts of law. As long as there are unethical or incompetent workers, and as long as competent and ethical workers can be challenged by a litigious public, there is need for professional "in-house" reviews.

Many workers seek to avoid sanctions by obstructing the work of the review panel. They attempt to do so by challenging the authority or jurisdiction of the review board, by threatening legal action against the board, and by refusing to cooperate. These actions do not aid the cause of the worker and usually lead to costly, embarrassing, and drawn out cases. If a worker refuses to cooperate, the likelihood is that the allegations of the complainant will be sustained.

TEN STEPS FOR AVOIDING AND MINIMIZING SANCTIONS

If a social worker is brought before a review panel, the goal is to prevent the authority from imposing punishment. If punishment cannot be avoided, the goal is to minimize its severity and duration. There are ten steps a worker should take to avoid or minimize sanctions by the professional review authority.

1. Become as knowledgeable as possible about the procedures of the relevant review organization and the overall standards of professional and ethical conduct. Continue to adhere to these standards after notification of the allegations.
2. Carefully evaluate the charges. Compare them with the explicit standards and relevant part of the code of ethics.
3. Consult one or more professional colleagues and obtain objective opinions about possible responses.
4. Seek professional legal counsel. Even though the lawyer may not be admitted to the panel hearing, the advice about conduct, procedures, legal recourse, and effective presentation of one's case can be invaluable.

5. Prepare a thoughtful, thorough, and truthful statement to explain and defend the actions which were alleged to be harmful to the complainant.

6. If, after investigation and review, the worker agrees with all or part of the allegations, the worker should admit fault and do so promptly. A prompt admission of allegations that have a substantial basis in fact, along with sincere contrition, is likely to result in less severe penalty.

7. If fault is admitted, the worker should then propose an appropriate sanction and agree to adhere to it. This may include financial restitution, written apology to the client, agreement to undertake therapy or supervision for a specified time, or to not engage in social work practice for a defined time. Proposing one's own punishment is likely to result in a more appropriate sanction and less negative publicity.

8. If the social worker disagrees with the allegations, the worker should nevertheless be cooperative with the review organization and present justifications in the most effective way possible. While the worker may be angry at the review panel, anger will accomplish nothing positive and may be detrimental to one's defense.

9. If a review panel sustains allegations and the appeals process affirms the sanctions imposed, the worker should accept it. In nearly all cases, contesting the action in courts of law will probably be futile, even if it is determined that some procedures were improper. Courts place confidence in peer review systems; attorneys and judges have been subject to very similar procedures.

10. Complete the penalty cooperatively. The goal here is redemption and renewed professional credibility. The most productive thing one can do is learn from this hard experience.

Chapter 9

Preparing for Litigation

Litigation is increasingly probable for social workers, just as it is for all other members of modern American society. The risk of being named as a defendant in a malpractice suit or a criminal action is no longer an unlikely, or even remote, prospect. There are also increased odds of having to fulfill the civic and professionally responsible obligation of providing testimony, either as an expert witness or as a direct observer of criminal or unethical activity.

Most social workers want to avoid these encounters, knowing that they can be costly, time-consuming, and professionally risky. Even winning a malpractice case will probably result in a considerable loss of money, prestige, time, and emotional security. Testifying against clients and colleagues will also be stressful, unpleasant, and time consuming and, if there are any rewards, they will be minimal and indirect.

Taking action in advance to minimize these risks has become not only prudent but essential. Doing so can significantly reduce the chances of being named in a malpractice case; it can also reduce the likelihood of negative consequences of losing one. Advanced preparation can keep down the time and money costs of litigation and remove some of the stress and diminution of prestige. The purpose of this chapter is to discuss some of the actions a social worker might take to prepare for litigation.

RECOGNIZING A POTENTIAL LEGAL HAZARD

The first step to be taken by a prudent social worker is to be alert to those situations that carry some risk of legal dispute. This in itself is often more difficult than it might seem. Professionals have almost always become inextricably involved in their legal situations before they are aware of the seriousness of their circumstances. The case of Mrs. W illustrates:

Mrs. W, a 27-year-old social worker with four years professional experience in a family service agency, was asked to testify before a grand jury. She had recently concluded treatment with the C family because of their failure to keep appointments. The worker had noted that Mr. C had a violent temper and was abusive to his wife and their eight-year-old child. On numerous occasions he had "spanked" the child so severely that medical care was needed.

On three occasions, the mother fled with the child to an emergency shelter. However, they kept returning. As the worker's notes indicated, the mother had symptoms of "learned helplessness," "masochistic tendencies," and "codependency" with her husband and his problems; the worker wrote that the mother's emotional problems led her to return repeatedly to her husband despite his behavior. The worker's diagnosis of Mr. C was "explosive personality," and "paranoid personality disorder."

Two months after the worker's last session with the Cs, their child died. It happened in a hospital, but was the result of internal bleeding and organ damage. In the investigation the parents both agreed he had fallen out of a tree and that they had taken him to the hospital immediately. The autopsy showed that the death was not caused by a fall but by various blows that had occurred a few days before the hospital admission.

The grand jury was trying to determine if the father and mother should be tried for the death. Mrs. W was one of their witnesses. Under oath, the social worker said she believed the father had been dangerous to the mother and child, and that she was trying to treat him for the condition; she indicated that the mother seemed to condone his behavior. The worker was then asked what she herself had done to notify the authorities about the danger. She said she discussed the matter with the physician who had treated the child for prior injuries; the physician said he had called Child Protective Services so there was no need for her to do likewise. There was no record of anyone having called CPS or any other authorities.

Before long, the worker found herself answering more questions about her own conduct in the case than she was answering about the

C family. Had she told her supervisors at the agency about how dangerous the client was? Had she told the doctor about what she had learned about both parents? Had she called any authorities? Had she followed up with the doctor to see if CPS was pursuing the case? Why did she not call CPS herself? Had she told Mrs. C. or the child where they could go or what they could do to avoid further risk? Had she terminated their treatment when they still needed help? Did she tell the doctor or any authorities that she had terminated with them?

The questions continued until it dawned on Mrs. W that she, too, had now become a subject of the investigation. She had answered many questions, on record under oath, without legal counsel before she realized she would be charged with a crime—that of failing to protect the child in grave peril as prescribed by law. Later, her attorney said her statements before the grand jury made her defense much more difficult. Eventually she was convicted. The father, who later admitted abusing the child, was found not guilty by reason of insanity.

OTHER POTENTIAL RISK SITUATIONS

Had Mrs. W known better about how to avoid or minimize legal risks, she might well have experienced a happier outcome. Her situation is one of the most common types of legal risk situations facing today's social workers—the failure to properly report "dangerous" clients to authorities and to take necessary actions to protect people from clients. Another serious risk is defamation—when a worker reports a client or colleague for apparently damaging behavior or suspected behavior, that person may be inclined to seek legal help to obtain damages. Other risk situations include testifying against colleagues or any former clients, dealing with litigious clients, and, of course, carrying out one's professional duties in unethical, improper, or criminal manners.

A relatively small proportion of social workers have been found guilty of crimes in the course of their professional activity. Only a few serious crimes have been reported in the media. The most prominent of these involved the worker who was sentenced to 25 years imprisonment after being convicted of murdering an elderly client and throwing her body in a river after taking her life's savings (*The New York Times,* 1979). Most other reported crimes by social workers have involved embezzlement and fraud against clients and third parties, and the practice of medicine without licenses. It should be needless to say the best way to avoid such legal risks is to always obey the law and carry out one's professional duties in an ethical and competent manner.

Dealing with litigious clients has become somewhat problematical for workers. A litigious client is one who has a proclivity for bringing actions to court. People most likely to fit this group are those who have initiated lawsuits in the past, especially against other professionals. People who have indicated a history of financial and personal disputes with others, especially professionals, may also be in this category. People who have been diagnosed as "paranoid," or "personality disordered" also tend toward litigiousness. People who fit this category are just as much in need of professional assistance as any other, and the conscientious worker will treat them too; however, the treatment should probably be fulfilled with great care and deliberate planning.

To reduce the legal risks of reporting dangerous clients to the authorities, one most know what the relevant laws are and what the appropriate procedures are for reporting. The relevant laws and statutes are available for direct reading in most libraries. Every state now has laws about reporting suspected child abuse. There is no excuse for a worker's ignorance about this (Bernstein, 1982). Nearly every state (and probably every state eventually) also has *Tarasoff*-type rulings which require workers to report their clients' intent to harm others. If the report is made cautiously and according to law the risks of criminal actions or defamation suits are reduced to the extent possible.

PROCEDURES FOR REPORTING

The legal risk of formally disclosing the behavior or suspected behavior of a client or colleague is reduced by doing so in a reasonable and cautious way, according to the standards established by those who have done it successfully. It is essential that the worker make the report to the right parties in a timely manner, providing accurate and truthful information without any personal opinions, embellishment, or motivations.

Determining who is the right party to receive the report is not always easy. Making it to the wrong party can result in the report getting lost or ignored. Or it can increase the risk of defamation suits. The right party to be notified depends on the nature of the case and people involved. If the worker has any reason to believe that anyone is in imminent danger of physical harm, a documented call to the local emergency authority (such as the 911 number) is essential. This could be done in the company of one's supervisor, agency employer, or other colleague. The action should be thoroughly noted in the client's case record and include the name of the official who received the call. If danger seems possible but not imminent, the worker may make several calls: the non-emergency police or sheriff number, the office of the prosecuting attorney, the local office of Child Protective Services (if a child is vulnerable), and the Department of Social Services.

To meet the requirement to notify an intended victim of one's client, even more caution is needed. Not only is there risk of defamation suits, but the client may turn the anger and threat toward the worker. In any event, timely action is essential. Workers have lost cases when they have delayed in making their reports for only a few days. The worker should discuss the situation with the supervisor or agency chief. This is partly for the supervisor's protection. According to the *respondeat superior* doctrine, the supervisor may be held liable for the actions or inactions of the worker. If the worker's supervisor advises against making calls of this type, it may be necessary to discuss the matter with others higher in the chain of command.

Workers who report colleagues for unethical or improper conduct, or testify against them in malpractice or ethics hearings, face other risks. If the worker is reporting on alleged unethical conduct by another professional, then the local professional association or licensing board is usually the place to call. This is most commonly done when a worker is told by a client about treatment the client endured while in the care of a previous worker. However, such calls should never be made by workers who have some personal dispute or grievance with the other professional. In this case the client should be referred to another worker who could then make the appropriate calls.

Social workers sometimes worry that their formal testimony against colleagues or former clients can result in legal problems. Actually these situations contain relatively less risk. One is not held liable for statements made under examination in courts of law. In formal hearings before professional or peer review boards, the danger of malpractice suits is also overblown (Qualliotine, 1991). If the worker reports only facts known about the colleague, a suit is unlikely. A defamation suit cannot be won if the allegations are true, and few lawyers would take such a case.

Some workers believe they will minimize legal risks simply by ignoring problems of these types. They plan to avoid potentially litigious clients, look the other way about colleague misconduct, and ignore the dangerousness that some clients seem to pose. Such behavior is unwise as well as socially and professionally irresponsible. These workers are failing in their duty to help protect vulnerable people and maintain the integrity of their profession. And their position makes them no less vulnerable in the long run because they have not prepared themselves emotionally or legally for the situations that may be inevitable.

DOCUMENTATION AND RECORD KEEPING

Any risks of legal problems are dramatically reduced when the worker has well-documented case records which truthfully indicate the rationale for whatever actions are taken. If the worker has a good reason for the professional action in the care and treatment of a client, and if that reason is noted, it would be exceedingly difficult to sustain a malpractice allegation against the worker, even if the treatment outcome was not desirable. Social workers usually have, or certainly should have, good reasons for the type of treatment they provide for their clients, but too often they fail to indicate what that reason is in the case record.

Legislation, third-party review, and judicial interpretations in recent years have meant that the professional person's case records are virtually part of the public record. In grand juries, courts of law, and other discovery procedures, the worker's record must now almost always be brought (*subpoena duces tecum*). This has presented some problems for social workers who fail to keep good records. It has also been a problem for professionals who work with groups or families. The case of the Y family illustrates:

Mr. and Mrs. Y sought marital therapy with a social worker to help them resolve their many personality conflicts and life-style disputes. Mr. Y preferred to stay at home and watch TV with the children, while Mrs. Y wanted to leave them with babysitters and participate in evening civic activities. Arguments in the worker's office about such matters were frequent. Mrs. Y occasionally exclaimed in frustration that she wished she had not had children so she could pursue her other interests better. Mr. Y claimed to be happy as he was.

A year after their marital therapy sessions ended, the Ys filed for divorce. A fight over custody of the children ensued. Mr. Y's attorney subpoenaed the worker and his client's case records. The worker, who personally believed that Mrs. Y was probably the more suitable parent for the children's upbringing, reviewed the records. There were no individual records for Mr. Y and Mrs. Y but only one for "The Y Family." In it information about both parties was intertwined — nearly every sentence had materials about both.

How, the worker wondered, could "Mr. Y's record" be brought to court without also including Mrs. Y's record. If information that the worker had recorded about her was included in testimony, it would unfairly harm her case and violate the worker's confidentiality pledge to her. The worker also contemplated deleting that part of the record that pertained to Mrs. Y. However, this would make the record incomprehensible and appear to have been improperly altered.

The worker explained this to Mr. Y's attorney who, more than ever, wanted the records brought to court. The worker then explained the situation to Mrs. Y and her attorney who emphatically did not want the records brought. Despite their protests at court the record was entered as evidence. Whether or not it influenced the outcome of the case was unknown, but Mr. Y won custody, and Mrs. Y felt her worker had weakened her case.

The worker tried thereafter to keep separate records for each individual client. This was a cumbersome process because in his particular specialty most of his clients were families and groups. The very premise of his treatment format was to use systems concepts, in which the behaviors of each family member influenced and were influenced by the behaviors of all other family members. It was not very satisfactory, but seemed better than the only alternative, that of altering any case records that henceforth were subpeonaed.

Social workers and other professionals have, all too often, embellished or otherwise changed their case records upon being required to take them to court. Usually they do this to document the work they failed to record while treating the client. They hope their legal risk situation will be reduced if the case record is more thorough than it was originally. However, this is highly risky and can result in criminal actions against the worker. It is far more sensible to maintain accurate and thorough ongoing records, even if it is time-consuming. The social work literature includes important information about how this recording process can be less time consuming and more useful for the worker and client, and help minimize legal problems (Kagle, 1991).

THE MENTAL-EMOTIONAL RISKS OF LITIGATION

One of the risks of legal problems that receives relatively less attention than it merits is the stress and mental toll that it exerts on workers. For social workers who testify in behalf of plaintiffs, the emotional turmoil and conflict is usually intense; for social workers who are defendants in criminal or malpractice cases, it is always enormous. The procedure usually takes months or years from the time of initial inquiries to ultimate resolution through court decisions or settlements. Prolonged stress is never healthy.

Nevertheless, there is only so much one can do to prepare for the emotional stress of litigation. It includes gaining as much knowledge as possible, developing and maintaining a strong support system, being prepared financially to the extent possible, and procuring the best available legal counsel possible. It starts by maintaining one's physical health. A visit to one's physician and discussion of the anticipated stress is in order. This may result in a physical examination, stress reducing medication, proper diet, and an exercise program.

Knowing about legal procedures, consequences, and possible outcomes will help reduce some stress. The fear of ultimate disaster can be mitigated by knowing more about what the actual consequences might be (best and worst case scenarios). Understanding routine courtroom procedures and discussing the situation with others who have experienced similar situations can also help. Merely sitting in on ongoing courtroom trials can remove some of the anxiety.

Many social workers who face malpractice or other legal problems are deprived of one of the things they need most, a strong support system. They fear disclosure will result in loss of respect from colleagues, clients, and even family. So they tend to conceal their plight and even avoid others. The opposite action is healthier and more effective. Unless their lawyers advise against it, they should openly discuss the case and their rationale in it with their colleagues, friends, and family. Doing so will help them understand their own actions better and will usually help them articulate their defenses better. A group of supporters who are loyal and respectful no matter what happens will help most workers endure the most difficult of circumstances.

FINANCIAL ASPECTS OF LITIGATION

Preparing for litigation also includes being ready for the economic costs that will accompany the situation. The process will be costly to the worker, even one who is well-covered by insurance. Costs only start with lawyer fees and expenses in connection with the actual defense. Less obvious costs include the inevitable losses of revenue that might be anticipated if the legal problem had not occurred. For example, the worker must take considerable time away from clients or agency service and this ultimately results in reduced income. It may also result in reduced chances for advancement and pay raises.

If the worker is well-covered against malpractice judgments, the costs are still painful. Premium fees for malpractice insurance will surely be raised. The worker is more likely to be dropped from future coverage and might have to seek coverage by independent insurance companies at far higher rates. Many policies do not in-

clude all the costs of the litigation. They might pay only for judgments made against the defendant-worker and not for the lawyer's
fees, or vice versa. Some workers find they are not covered if they
have also been found to have broken the law. Many insurance companies are not required to pay if they find any misrepresentation by
the worker on the application. A professional would be extremely
unwise to make a false statement on such an insurance form, no
matter how unimportant it might seem at first.

The other significant cost of legal problems will be legal counsel.
The seriousness of the situation is such that a worker can ill afford
not to obtain the best possible representation. This does not mean
the most expensive lawyer, necessarily; but conversely, it does not
imply trying to save expenses with the cheapest counsel either. It
means that the worker should, with great care and thoughtfulness,
employ the most effective lawyer possible.

EMPLOYING AN EFFECTIVE LAWYER

Obtaining effective legal representation — the right lawyer for this
particular case — is most important single activity the worker in such
circumstances can do. As every case and social worker's situation is
unique, so too is the experience, expertise, and resources of every
attorney. The challenge for the social worker is to make the right
match.

To do so, several questions must be answered: When should a
lawyer be consulted and when is it unnecessary? At what point in
the case progression is the lawyer employed? How is the most suitable one found? What is the most effective way to assist the lawyer
to make the best case possible? How can legal costs and lawyer fees
be contained?

WHEN TO SEEK LEGAL HELP

Knowing when to consult an attorney should be thought out in
advance. No social worker could hire an attorney every time there is
a potential practice-related legal problem, but one's case could be
seriously weakened by waiting too long. Clearly, a lawyer should
always be consulted when the worker is charged with a crime,

named in a lawsuit, or contacted by a client's lawyer about the possibility of legal action. Also, it is usually advisable to seek legal representation before giving information to grand juries, prosecutors, or other law officials about any case in which the worker or worker's employing agency could become named as a defendant.

In most cases it will not be necessary to consult a lawyer whenever a client first threatens legal action, or when a worker is testifying in court as an expert witness or in court in behalf of a client. Experienced social workers recognize that threats of lawsuit are frequently made hastily and withdrawn when the intended intimidation is not forthcoming. Social workers are generally not vulnerable to legal problems as a result of their own testimony if their words are truthful and their opinions are requested in court and based on established expertise. However, if the direction of the testimony moves toward alleged wrongdoing by the worker, it is time to resist further self-disclosure and seek an attorney's advice at the first opportunity.

There are always going to be gray areas and exceptions to whatever criteria are set out in advance. If in doubt, it is better to err on the side of caution and seek the attorney's assistance than to ignore potential problems and hope for the best. Many experienced social workers, especially those who work in highly sensitive areas such as child protection services, maintain professional relationships with lawyers so that they can have ready access whenever faced with gray-area situations. Also, most social agencies have ongoing relationships with attorneys who are consulted whenever a potential legal problem occurs. However, the individual worker's interest may not always be synonymous with that of the agency; seeking additional legal representation in such cases is often wise.

At what point in the case progression is the lawyer called upon? The goal here is to get legal representation before potential risk begins to escalate, but to avoid premature haste and panic. If there is some risk, the attorney should be called whenever the worker is asked for information which is potentially harmful. Disclosing such information should never occur without the attorney's concurrence. This point may vary according to the seriousness of the problem for the worker. The general rule is: the higher the degree of legal risk, the sooner the right lawyer should be consulted.

CHOOSING THE RIGHT LAWYER

Finding the best lawyer for the particular case involves much more than looking through the yellow pages or watching television advertisements. First, it is important to determine whether to employ a specialist or a generalist. A specialist will usually be more effective than a generalist who is not well-versed in the relevant aspects of the issue to be adjudicated. A specialist in criminal law is essential if the worker is charged with a crime. Specialists in malpractice litigation should also be consulted for most types of potential malpractice suits.

Generally, it is better to employ a lawyer who practices in the area where the case is going to be heard rather than to retain an outsider. A lawyer who is part of a large law firm may be more expensive, but with the firm's research and other resources, the case might be handled more efficiently. However, if the lawyer in the larger firm cannot devote the attention needed to the case, or delegates much of the work to others, it might be advantageous to employ the services of a lawyer in a smaller firm. Many legal scholars advise that well-qualified but hungrier and more energetic younger lawyers may be able to do more for the worker in a malpractice suit than would the so-called "biggest and best" lawyers or firms in the area.

Once one has an idea of the type of lawyer needed, locating that person can be more focused. A list of possible lawyers should be compiled. This is done by consulting colleagues who have encountered similar situations, and by asking other lawyers who are not candidates for the job. These lawyers can be those previously known to the worker, attorneys who have provided personal legal services for the worker or the worker's clients, or lawyers with whom the worker has served in civic activities.

Other names can be added to the list by contacting lawyer referral services, as long as they are sponsored by the local bar associations. Those referral services without such sponsorship are often no more reliable then yellow page listings. Legal directories, such as the *Martindale-Hubbell Law Directory,* the *Attorney's Register,* the *Directory of the Legal Profession,* and local directories also may be useful. They specify each lawyer's type of expertise and experience. They are available in most larger community libraries and in every law school library.

RETAINING THE LAWYER

Before the lawyer is retained, the social worker should find out if the lawyer is qualified to manage the case, is available at the time needed, has experience in similar cases, and has any potential conflicts of interest. If satisfied so far, the worker should also determine how the lawyer would attempt to handle the case, what is the estimated time before resolution, and how much of the work would be done by the lawyer and how much by associates.

If this is satisfactory, the social worker also needs to know in advance about the financial arrangement, especially whether the requirement is based on an hourly fee, a flat payment for specified services, or on some contingency. The social worker should also request references from the lawyer and ask those people if they were satisfied with the lawyer's handling of their cases.

The worker should only employ a lawyer who provides satisfactory references, fee arrangements and billing procedures, and assurances about devoting enough time to the case to be effective. The lawyer should agree to regular (monthly or quarterly) billing that is detailed, rather than an overall summary. Finally, the social worker needs to know how the lawyer will provide information about the case as it develops.

When the agreement is made to employ the lawyer, the terms should be delineated in an engagement letter. This is accompanied by a nonreturnable retainer fee that may be paid in advance. This fee is to cover costs up to a certain point in the case before regular billing begins. Of course the lawyer should also agree to refund any part of the retainer that is not used. Most lawyers charge by the hour and should itemize their time along with their bills.

Costs can be minimized if the worker assists the lawyer in an effective way and avoids such inefficiencies as needlessly telephoning the lawyer for information about minutia or to gain more reassurance. Other efficiencies include doing most of the communicating by telephone instead of office visits, and providing all the information requested by the lawyer in an organized fashion.

When the lawyer and social worker begin their efforts together on the case, the most effective approach is that of teamwork, with the lawyer serving as team leader. The social worker serves on that team with an attitude of trust, candor, and cooperativeness. This improves the likelihood that legal problems for the worker will be minimized. In such a way the professions of social work and the law can be effective in meeting their mutual interests and those of society.

Glossary of Forensic Social Work Terms

Forensic social workers have a language all their own. The language derives from law terms as well as the vocabulary of social workers. Language and nomenclature center around the words that social workers use in legal situations such as courtroom testimony, obtaining admissible evidence, public regulation, malpractice, professional review, and accountability. The following are definitions of some of the most important terms used in forensic social work, many of which are referred to in this book. Additional relevant terms for forensic social work may be found in Robert L. Barker (1991a) *The Social Work Dictionary, 2nd Edition,* Silver Spring, MD: National Association of Social Workers.

abandonment: Relinquishing one's rights, obligations, or possessions voluntarily, with no intention of subsequently reclaiming them. Abandonment of one's family may be used as grounds for divorce or loss of child custody in most states.

abduction: Transporting someone, often by force, coercion, or deception, against that person's will; or, if the person is a child or mentally incompetent, doing so without the consent of the parent or legal guardian.

adoption: Taking a person, usually a child or infant, into one's home and treating him or her as though born into the family. The legal process involves changing court records to show the legal transfer from the birth parents to the adopting parents. Adoption gives the individual the same rights of inheritance as other children and the adoptive parents the same responsibilities and rights of control as other parents.

adjudication: A court decision and the process of reaching that decision through a legal hearing or trial.

adversarial process: A procedure for reaching decisions by hearing and evaluating the presentation of opposing viewpoints. See also **ex parte process.**

alimony: See **maintenance.**

amnesty: An excuse granted to individuals or groups to free them from being tried or punished for criminal offenses.

appeal: A request of a higher court to review and reverse a lower court decision or grant a new trial. This higher court is called an appellate court. Its function is limited to determining if judgments made in lower courts were made in accordance with the law. Appellate courts review only written briefs and oral arguments about how the previous judgment came to be made and do not review new testimony or evidence.

assault: An attempt or threat that creates in another the reasonable apprehension of imminent harmful or offensive bodily contact. Assault may be found even where no physical injury occurs if the victim has been subjected to a reasonable fear of harm or offensive contact. When such force through physical contact occurs, the term is called **battery.**

bail: A monetary or other form of security posted by or for someone accused of a crime. The purpose is to ensure that the accused will appear at subsequent legal proceedings, to enable the accused to avoid imprisonment while awaiting trial, and to relieve the authorities of the costs of incarcerating the accused during this period.

battery: Unlawful harmful or offensive bodily contact with another. The terms "battered child" and "battered spouse" refer to victims of this crime.

cease and desist order: A statement made by a court or judicial authority prohibiting an individual or organization from starting or continuing a particular activity. Similar terms are injunction, temporary restraining order, preliminary injunction, and protective order.

child abuse: Inflicting physical or emotional injury on a dependent minor through intentional beatings, uncontrolled corporal punishment, persistent ridicule and degradation, or sexual abuse, usually committed by parents or others in charge of the child's care.

child neglect: The failure of those responsible for the care of a minor to provide the resources needed for healthy physical, emotional, and social development. Examples of neglect include inadequate nutrition, improper supervision, deficient health care, and not providing for educational requirements.

child molestation: A form of child abuse involving forcing a child to participate in some sexual activity; i.e., behaviors that can include rape, incest, erotic fondling, or compelling the child to behave in a way that erotically stimulates the perpetrator.

class action suit: A civil legal action taken by or on behalf of a group, community, or members of a social entity against an alleged perpetrator of harm to that group or some of its members.

clemency: An official grant from the highest legal officer which forgives an individual from liability or punishment for specified criminal acts. Clemency differs from amnesty in that it applies to specific crimes and people rather than classes of people.

code of ethics: An explicit statement of the values, principles, and rules of a profession that regulate the conduct of its members.

commitment: Consigning an individual to a hospital or prison, usually after undergoing due process of law.

community property: Assets jointly owned by a husband and wife by the fact of their marriage. In states that have community property laws, both spouses are generally considered by law to equally share all property either has acquired during the marriage, but not before the marriage.

community service sentence: Punishment for a crime imposed by courts of law requiring a convicted person to perform some activity for the social good in lieu of imprisonment. Typically the crimes are nonviolent and the duties often consist of working a specified number of hours in such settings as homeless shelters, social agencies, hospitals, and inner city recreation centers.

competence: The ability to fulfill the requirements of an obligation and the capacity to understand and act reasonably.

competent evidence: The convincing, reliable, valid, and relevant facts about a case that are admissible in courts of law, as distinguished from the opinions, guesses, or secondhand data.

conservator: A court appointed guardian or custodian of the assets belonging to someone who is incompetent to manage them properly.

contempt of court: Behavior that interferes with the administration of justice or shows disrespect for the dignity and authority of the court. Such behavior may occur within the courtroom during a trial (known as direct contempt) or outside (constructive contempt). Such behavior is punishable by fine or, to a limited extent, imprisonment.

contributing to the delinquency of a minor: The crime by parents, legal guardians, or others who have influence with a child, of facilitating unlawful behavior in that child, through neglect, coercion, example, or encouragement. These actions include permitting the youngster to avoid school, to stay out late at night, to consume alcohol and drugs, and to be exposed to unlawful activities by the parents.

custody: A legal right and obligation of a person or group to possess, control, protect, or maintain guardianship over some designated property or over another person who is unable to function autonomously (for example, children and certain disabled adults).

custody of children: A legal determination in divorce cases specifying which parent or other guardian will be in charge of the child. The court awards custody to the mother or father who is deemed most likely to promote the best interests of the child. This parent is called the "custodial parent," and thereby has the ultimate responsibility for the care and control of the child. In some circumstances joint or shared custody is awarded so that both parents retain responsibility. Typically in joint custody the child lives with each parent for a fixed period of time and both parents are equally responsible for all relevant decisions regarding the child's upbringing.

defamation: Written or spoken false statements about a person which cause harm. This term is now preferred over the terms **libel** (written statements causing harm) and **slander** (spoken statements causing harm).

default judgment: A decision made against a defendant who fails to appear for a court hearing, after due notice has been given and the statutory periods of responses have elapsed.

double jeopardy: Being subjected to prosecution and trial a second time for the same offense. Freedom from this is guaranteed by the Fifth Amendment of the U.S. Constitution.

due process: Adherence to all the rules, procedures, protections, opportunities, and considerations of fairness legally available when a person accused of a crime or offense is brought to trial or hearing involving possible deprivation of life, liberty, or property.

Durham rule: The 1954 court decision declaring that if a person's unlawful act was the product of mental disease then the accused is not criminally responsible.

ex parte process: A legal proceeding in which, because of urgent concerns involving the welfare of a child or likelihood of irreparable damage to a person or property, a court grants relief after hearing only one side of the dispute. See also **adversarial process.**

expert witness: One who testifies before a court or lawmaking group, based on special knowledge of the subject in question, which can result in a better assessment of the evidence or merits of the case.

expunge: A legal procedure in which certain records about an individual are destroyed. In many jurisdictions some juveniles may have records pertaining to delinquent acts expunged upon reaching adulthood. Individuals who have been arrested unlawfully or not convicted may apply to have their arrest records expunged.

family court: A court of law that hears cases pertaining to conflicts among family members, such as divorce, custody, adoption, or support matters. Often cases involving juvenile delinquency are also heard in such courts.

garnishment: A legal process in which a debtor's money or other property (such as wages, salary, or savings) in the possession of another person is applied to a debt owed to another third party. Due process requires that the debtor be given notice and an opportunity to be heard by a court which may order the employer, banker, or other holder of the property to remit such funds to an agent of the court or to the person to whom the money is owed until the obligation has been fulfilled.

Gault decision: The 1967 U.S. Supreme Court decision that affirmed the right of juveniles to the same legal protections as are given adults in criminal court proceedings, including advance notification of charges, right to counsel, freedom from self-incrimination, and the opportunity to have counsel confront witnesses.

Gideon v. Wainright: The 1963 U.S. Supreme Court ruling that all indigent defendants in criminal cases involving imprisonment have the right to free legal counsel.

grievance committee: A formal group established to evaluate whether an organization's policies and activities have resulted in harm to a complainant, to recommend changes in the policy/activity which have been deemed harmful, and to recommend ways to make amends for those harmed. Grievance committees are usually comprised of members of the organization.

guardian: One who has the legal responsibility for the care and management of a child or incompetent adult. *Guardian ad litem* refers to a temporary guardian, an officer of the court appointed by the court to manage the affairs of another for a specified time.

habeas corpus: The legal right of an individual who is held in a prison or other institution to appear before the judge so that there can be a determination whether that person is being held in violation of constitutional rights to due process.

hearsay evidence: Statements made by witnesses in courts of law based, not on their direct observation, but on what they heard others say; it is offered to prove the truth of the matter stated.

implied consent: An agreement to participate as expressed by gestures, signs, nonresisting silence, or inaction. This is often used as a defense in rape trials in which the defendant claims to have acted in the belief that the victim consented to his advances.

impound: To seize or attack funds, records, or property by an officer of the law or court, usually until some matter which involves those items can be legally adjudicated.

incapacitation: Lack of ability to provide sufficient care or judgment for oneself, due to diminished physical or mental functioning.

indictment: A sworn, written accusation presented by a grand jury to the court charging a person with a felony.

informed consent: The client's granting of permission to the professional and agency to use specific intervention procedures, including diagnosis, treatment, followup, and research. This permission must be based on full disclosure of the facts needed to make the decision intelligently. Informed consent must be based on knowledge of the risks and alternatives.

incompetent: Without ability to fulfill obligations. In a legal sense this term refers to inability to consent legally to make or execute a contract, insufficient knowledge needed to carry out some legal obligation, unfitness to stand trial because of inability to assist in one's own defense, or inability to understand the nature of the charge or the consequences of conviction.

in loco parentis: A relationship involving the legally sanctioned assumption of parental responsibilities of a child or incompetent adult without a formal adoption. Such relationships most commonly exist when a child is in a residential institution, reformatory, or boarding school.

insanity: A legal term used to indicate the presence of a severe mental disorder, which negates the individual's responsibility for certain acts, including criminal conduct. The person declared legally insane is thought to lack substantial capacity either to appreciate the wrongfulness of a criminal act or to act in conformity with the requirements of the law.

insanity plea: See **McNaughten Rule.**

intestate: Having died without leaving a valid will.

legal aid: The provision of free or reduced fee legal counsel to a litigant who cannot afford a private attorney.

libel: Written false statements about a person which cause harm. See also **defamation.**

litigation: Disputes contested in courts of law. A litigant is one who is actively involved in a lawsuit either as a defendant or plaintiff. A litigious client is one who indicates a predisposition to initiate lawsuits.

maintenance: Money paid to an ex-spouse by the other in accordance with legal requirements to provide for independent living expenses. Maintenance is the modern term for **alimony** and is distinct from the obligation of child support payments.

malpractice: Behavior by a professional person in the course of his or her job involving a failure of the person to bring to the matter at hand that amount of care, skill, and knowledge possessed by the ordinary reasonable professional in that or similar communities, resulting in harm to the client.

McNaughten Rule: A set of legal principles for the guidance of courts in helping to determine if a defendant may be declared not guilty by reason of insanity. Based on the 1843 British case of Daniel McNaughten, the court considers the accused not responsible for the crime he or she committed if a mental disease rendered the person unable to know the nature or quality of the act or that it was wrong to do. Many jurisdictions use different criteria. For example, the American Law Institute's formulation states that "a person is not responsible for criminal conduct if at the time of such conduct as a result of mental disease or defect he lacks substantial capacity either to appreciate the wrongfulness of his conduct or to conform his conduct to the requirements of law."

Miranda rule: The 1966 U.S. Supreme Court ruling, in *Miranda v. Arizona,* requiring police to inform suspects of their constitutional rights before questioning them.

neglect: Failure to meet one's legal or moral obligations or duties, especially to dependent family members. When such conduct results in harm or potential harm to others, legal proceedings may be taken to compel the person to meet the relevant obligations or face punishment.

negligence: Failure to exercise reasonable care or caution, resulting in another person being subjected to harm or unwarranted risk of harm; also failure to fulfill responsibility that is necessary to protect or help another.

parens patriae: The legal doctrine that refers to the role of the state as the guardian of people who are unable to care for themselves. The concept is most often used in courts in deciding to intervene in family matters, such as custody of children, divorce disputes, and removal of children to foster homes.

paternity suit: A legal proceeding to determine whether or not a particular man is the father of a child.

plea bargain: Negotiation between a prosecutor and a person accused of a crime, resulting in a disposition of the case. Typically the accused agrees to plead guilty to a lesser charge and forgoes a jury trial. The advantage to the accused is that the case is resolved sooner and at less risk of serious penalty. The advantages to the public are that court dockets are less backlogged and cases can be resolved with less cost.

plagiarism: Appropriating the scientific or literary writings of another person and presenting it as one's own work.

prenuptial agreement: A contract entered into by two people who plan to marry, delineating the rights and obligations of each in the event of divorce, annulment, or death.

pro bono publico: "For the good of the public," the Latin phrase, often shortened to *pro bono*, refers to a professional person (usually a lawyer) providing services at no charge to a needy recipient, especially one whose case has broader social implications.

protective custody: The placement of an individual by the legal authorities in a facility to prevent the person from danger of harm by others or from self-inflicted injury.

public defender: A state-supported attorney for persons who are accused of crimes but are unable to pay for their own counsel.

rape: The criminal act of forcing a nonconsenting person to engage in some form of sexual contact. The force may take the form of violent assault or real or implied threat. In "statutory rape," the sexual relationship involves a person who consents but who is below the legal age of consent.

***respondeat superior* doctrine:** Liability of employers or supervisors for the job-related actions of their employees.

restraining order: A temporary decree made by a judge or other legal authority without a prior hearing, prohibiting an individual or organization from performing some action pending an outcome of a later trial or hearing. An injunction differs in that it is made only after a formal hearing and has a permanent character to it.

right to refuse treatment: The legal principle, upheld in numerous court cases, that an individual may not be compelled to undergo any form of treatment, unless there is a life-threatening emergency or the person exhibits seriously destructive behavior.

right to treatment: The legal principle, established in the 1971 *Wyatt v. Stickney* decision, that an individual who is confined to an institution has the right to receive the treatment necessary to offer a reasonable chance for improvement so that the person can function independently and gain release from that institution.

search warrant: An order by a judge authorizing specified law officers to examine a subject's premises or possessions to bring them to the court. Search warrants can be issued only if there is probable cause to believe a crime has been committed and must particularly describe the place to be searched and the items or persons to be seized. The U.S. Constitution, Fourth Amendment, guarantees citizens freedom from unreasonable searches or seizures.

slander: Spoken false statements that damage the reputation of another person. See also **defamation.**

subpoena: A legal order requiring the individual to appear in court at a specified time. A *subpoena duces tecum* is one that requires the witness to bring to the court or deposition any relevant documents or materials possessed.

***Tarasoff* decision:** The 1976 ruling by the Supreme Court of California stating that, under certain circumstances, psychotherapists whose clients tell them that they intend to harm someone are obliged to warn the intended victim. Subsequently this decision has been adopted by courts and legislatures in many other states.

test case: A lawsuit to determine whether a law or legal practice is valid.

tort: A civil wrong that harms someone for which the injured party has the right to sue for damages in civil courts. Examples include malpractice, defamation, and negligence. Crimes and breaches of contract are not considered torts.

victim compensation: Public payment to people who are judged to have been harmed as a result of another's negligence or criminal conduct. When the perpetrator of the crime pays the victim the term is "restitution."

white collar crime: Nonviolent crimes by individuals or business organizations, usually committed in the course of the offender's occupation. The most frequent of these crimes include embezzlement, fraud, forgery, theft of property, fraudulent use of credit cards, stock manipulation, securities fraud, and other violations of trust.

Bibliography

Albert, R. (1986). *Law and Social Work Practice.* New York: Springer.

Alexander, R. (1989). "The Right to Treatment in Mental and Correctional Institutions." *Social Work.* 34:2. March. 109.

American Home Assurance Co. (1987). *Report on Claims Against Social Workers and Agencies.* New York: American Home Assurance Co.

Anderson, P. and L. Winfree (1987). *Expert Witnesses.* Albany, NY: State University of New York Press.

Antler, S. (1985). "Policy Statement on Social Worker Liability." *Child Welfare at the Crossroads: Professional Liability.* Silver Spring, MD: National Association of Social Workers.

Antler, S. (1987). "Professional Liability and Malpractice." *Encyclopedia of Social Work, 18th Edition.* Silver Spring, MD: National Association of Social Workers. 346.

Ashford, J.B., M.W. Macht, and M. Mylym (1987). "Advocacy by Social Workers in the Public Defenders Office." *Social Work.* 32:2 May-June. 199.

Barker, R.L. (1984). "The Tarasoff Paradox: Confidentiality and the Duty to Warn." *Social Thought.* Fall. 187.

Barker, R.L. (1982). *The Business of Psychotherapy.* New York: Columbia University Press. 207-209.

Barker, R.L. (1986). "Spelling Out the Rules and Goals: The Written Worker-Client Contract." *Journal of Independent Social Work.* 1:2. 67.

Barker, R.L. (1989). "Independent Social Workers and Legal Training." *Journal of Independent Social Work.* 3:3. 2.

Barker, R.L. (1990). "Mandatory Continuing Education: A Neglected Component of Competent Practice." *Journal of Independent Social Work.* 4:3. 3.

Barker, R.L. (1991a). *The Social Work Dictionary, 2nd Edition.* Silver Spring, MD: National Association of Social Workers.

Barker, R.L. (1991b). *Social Work in Private Practice, 2nd Edition.* Silver Spring, MD: National Association of Social Workers.

Barth, R.P. and R. Sullivan (1985). "Collecting Competent Evidence in Behalf of Children." *Social Work.* 30:2. March-April. 130.

Berliner, A.K. (1989). "Misconduct in Social Work Practice." *Social Work.* 34:1. January. 69.

Berman, A.L. (1990). "Standard of Care in Assessment of Suicidal Potential." *Psychotherapy in Private Practice.* 8:2. 35.

Bernstein, B.E. (1978). "Malpractice: An Ogre on the Horizon." *Social Work.* 23:2. March. 106.

Bernstein, B.E. (1981). "Malpractice: Future Shock of the 1980s." *Social Casework.* 62. March. 172.

Bernstein, B.E. (1982). *Ignorance of the Law Is No Excuse: Values, Ethics, Legalities, and the Family Therapist.* L. L'Abate, editor. Rockville, MD: Aspen Publications. 87.

Besharov, D.J. (1983). *Criminal and Civil Liability in Child Welfare Work: The Growing Trend.* Washington, DC: American Bar Association.

Besharov, D.J. (1985). *The Vulnerable Social Worker: Liability for Serving Children and Families.* Silver Spring, MD: National Association of Social Workers.

Besharov, D.J. and S.H. Besharov (1987). "Teaching about Liability." *Social Work.* 32:6. Nov-Dec. 517.

Borenzweig, H. (1977). "Who Passes the California Licensing Examination?" *Social Work.* 22:3 May. 173.

Branson, D.M. (1986). "Protecting and Fostering the Growth of a Successful Business Entity." Chapter 4 in *Washington Bar Association, Representing New or Expanding Businesses.* Seattle: Washington Bar Association. 86.

Branson, D.M. (1988). "Counseling the Board of Directors." Chapter 10 in *Washington Bar Association, Attorney-Client Relationships.* Seattle: Washington Bar Association. 217.

Branson, D.M. (1990). "Derivative Litigation." Chapter 4 in *Basic*

Corporate Practice. Seattle: University of Washington School of Law. 53.

Brieland, D. and J.A. Lemmon (1985). *Social Work and the Law.* St. Paul, MN: West Publishing Co.

Brieland, D. and S.Z. Goldfarb (1987). "Legal Issues and Legal Services." *Encyclopedia of Social Work, 18th Edition.* Silver Spring, MD: National Association of Social Workers. 28.

Brodsky, S. (1988). "Fear of Litigation in Mental Health Professionals." *Criminal Justice and Behavior.* 15(4). 492.

Brown, J.A., P.A. Unsinger, and M.W. More (1990). *Law Enforcement and Social Welfare: The Emergency Response.* Springfield, IL: Charles C Thomas Co.

Bullis, R.K. (1990). "Cold Comfort from the Supreme Court: Limited Liability Protection for Social Workers." *Social Work.* 35(4). July. 364.

Butler, J.D. and D.F. Walbert (1986). *Abortion, Medicine and the Law, Third Edition.* New York: Facts on File. 124.

Chandler, S.M. "Mediation: Conjoint Problem Solving." *Social Work.* 30:4. July-August. 346.

Cohen, R. (1979). *Malpractice: A Guide for Mental Health Practitioners.* New York: Free Press.

Coulton, C. (1987). "Quality Assurance." *Encyclopedia of Social Work, 18th Edition.* Silver Spring, MD. National Association of Social Workers. 443.

Croxton, T. (1988). "Caveats on Contracts." *Social Work.* 33(2). March/April. 169.

Curran, W.J., A.L. McGarry, and S.A. Shah (1986). *Forensic Psychiatry and Psychology.* Philadelphia, PA: F.A. Davis.

Dickson, D.T. (1976). "Law in Social Work: Impact of Due Process." *Social Work.* 20:4. July. 274.

deYoung, M. (1986). "A Conceptual Model for Judging the Truthfulness of a Young Child's Allegation of Sexual Abuse." *American Journal of Orthopsychiatry.* XLI: 1.38.

Dillon, K.M. (1987). "False Sexual Abuse Allegations: Causes and Concerns." *Social Work.* 32:6. November December. 540.

Dolan, M. (1988). "Preparing Social Workers for Licensing Exams." *Journal of Independent Social Work.* 3:2. 23.

Dubin, S.S. (1981). "Obsolescence or Lifelong Education: A

Choice for the Professional." *American Psychologist.* 81:6 June. 486

Duquette, D.N. (1990). *Advocating for the Child in Protection Proceedings.* Lexington, MA: Lexington Books.

Ennis, B. and L. Siegal (1982). *The Rights of Mental Patients: An American Civil Liberties Union Handbook.* New York: Avon Books.

Fatis, M. and others (1982). "Written Contracts as Adjuncts in Family Therapy." *Social Work.* 27:2 March/April. 169.

Flynn, J.P. (1987). "Licensing and Regulation of Social Work Services," *Encyclopedia of Social Work, 18th Edition."* Silver Spring, MD: National Association of Social Workers.

Ginsberg, L. (1990). "Selected Statistical Review." *Encyclopedia of Social Work, 18th Edition.* 1990 Supplement. Silver Spring, MD:NASW Press.

Gothard, S. (1987). "Juvenile Justice System." *Encyclopedia of Social Work, 18th Edition.* Silver Spring, MD: National Association of Social Workers. 5.

Gothard, S. (1989a). "Power in the Court: The Social Worker as an Expert Witness." *Social Work.* 34:1. 65.

Gothard, S. (1989b). "Rules of Testimony and Evidence for Social Workers Who Appear as Expert Witnesses in Courts of Law." *Journal of Independent Social Work.* 3:3. 7.

Gothard, S. (1991). Personal Correspondence with the authors. November 12.

Gross, S.J. (1978). "The Myth of Professional Licensing." *American Psychologist.* 78: 11. November. 672.

Gumz, E. (1987). *Professionals and Their Work in the Family Divorce Court.* Springfield, IL: Charles C Thomas.

Hahn, A.P. (1989). "Private Social Work Practice in a Legal Setting." *Journal of Independent Social Work.* 3:3. 17.

Handler, E. (1976). "Social Work and Corrections: Comments on an Uneasy Partnership." *Criminology.* 13:2. 240.

Hardcastle, D.A. (1990). "The Legal Regulation of Social Workers." *Encyclopedia of Social Work. 18th Edition,* 1990 Supplement. Silver Spring, MD: National Association of Social Workers. 203.

Hartman, A. (1990). "A Profession Chasing Its Tail—Again." *Social Work.* 35:2. March. 99.

Herrman, R. (1980). "Consumer Protection: Yesterday, Today, and Tomorrow." *Current History.* 78. 457.

Ivanov, A.M. (1987). "Suicide." *Encyclopedia of Social Work, 18th Edition.* Silver Spring, MD: National Association of Social Workers. 737.

Iverson, R.R. (1987). "Licensure: Help or Hindrance to Women Social Workers." *Social Casework.* 68:4. April. 271.

Jackson, J.A. (1987). "Clinical Social Work and Peer Review: A Professional Leap Ahead." *Social Work.* 32:3. May-June. 213.

Johnson, D.A. and D. Huff (1987). "Licensing Exams: How Valid Are They?" *Social Work.* 32:2. March-April. 159.

Kadushin, A. (1987). "Child Welfare Services." *Encyclopedia of Social Work, 18th Edition.* Silver Spring, MD: National Association of Social Workers. 265.

Kagle, J.D. (1991). *Social Work Records, 2nd Edition.* Homewood, IL: Dorsey Press.

Klier, J., E. Fein and C. Genero (1984). "Are Written or Verbal Contracts More Effective in Family Therapy?" *Social Work.* 29: 3. May-June. 264.

Koopman, E.J. and E.J. Hunt (1988). "Child Custody Mediation: An Interdisciplinary Synthesis." *American Journal of Orthopsychiatry.* 58:3. 379.

Korelitz, A. and D. Schulter (1982). "The Lawyer-therapist Consultation Team." *Journal of Marital and Family Therapy.* 8:1. 113.

Krause, H.D. (1986). *Family Law in a Nutshell, 2nd Edition.* St. Paul, MN: West Publishing Co.

Kutchins, H. and S.A. Kirk (1987). "DSM-III and Social Work Malpractice." *Social Work* 32:3 May-June. 205.

Land, H. (1987). "The Effects of Licensure on Student Motivation and Career Choice." *Social Work.* 32:1 January-February. 75.

Landers, S. (1992). "Social work now regulated across nation." *NASW News* 37,(6) June. p. 1.

Lindenthal, J.J., T.J. Jordan, J.D. Lentz, and C.S. Thomas (1988). "Social Workers' Management of Confidentiality." *Social Work.* 33:2. March-April. 157.

Lytle-Vieira, J.E. (1987). *"Kramer vs. Kramer* Revisited: The Social Work Role in Child Custody Cases." *Social Work.* 32:1. January-February. 61.

Macchiarola, F.J. (1988). "Not for Profit Organizations and the Liability Crisis." *Proceedings of the Academy of Political Science.* 37:10. 889.

Marcus, L.J. (1987). "Health Care Financing." *Encyclopedia of Social Work, 18th Edition.* Silver Spring, MD: National Association of Social Workers. 697.

Masters, W. and V. Johnson (1970). *Human Sexual Inadequacy.* Boston: Little, Brown and Co.

Meloy, J.R. (1987). "The Prediction of Violence in Outpatient Psychotherapy." *American Journal of Psychotherapy.* XLI:1. 462.

Melton, G. (1986). "Litigation in the Interests of Children: Does Anyone Win?" *Law and Human Behavior.* 10:4. 337.

Middleman, R.R. (1984). "How Competent Is Social Work's Approach to Assessment of Competence?" *Social Work.* 29:3. March-April. 141.

Middleton, M. (1982). "Red Tape Cutters: Social Workers Carve Out a Role." *American Bar Association Journal.* 69:579.

Miller, P. (1990). "Covenant Model for Professional Relationships: An Alternative to the Contract Model." *Social Work.* 35:2. March. 121.

Miller, R.D. and G.J. Maier (1990). "Factors Affecting the Decision to Prosecute Mental Patients in Criminal Behavior," in D.B. Wexler, ed., *Therapeutic Jurisprudence: The Law as a Therapeutic Agent.* Durham, NC: Carolina Academic Press. 369.

Miller, R.D., G.J. Maier, F.W. Blancke, and D. Doren (1990). "Litigiousness as a Resistance to Therapy," in D.B. Wexler, ed., *Therapeutic Jurisprudence: The Law as a Therapeutic Agent.* Durham, NC: Carolina Academic Press. 369-379.

NASW Chapter Guide (1980). *NASW Chapter Guide for the Adjudication of Grievances, Revised Edition.* Silver Spring, MD: National Association of Social Workers.

NASW (1981). National Association of Social Workers Standards for Social Work Practice in Child Protection. Silver Spring, MD: National Association of Social Workers.

NASW (1991). The NASW Code of Ethics, Revised Version, 1991. Silver Spring, MD: National Association of Social Workers.

The New York Times (1979). "The Social Worker Ordered to Prison for 25 Years in Murder of Client." September 11. PB3:5.

Osman, S. and S.A. Shueman (1988). "A Guide to the Peer Review Process for Clinicians." *Social Work.* 33:4. July-August. 345.

Patru, E. (1989). "Social Workers as Expert Witnesses (Letters)." *Social Work.* 34:3. May. 273.

Perlman, G.L. (1988). "Mastering the Law of Privileged Communication: A Guide for Social Workers." *Social Work.* 33:5. September-October. 425.

Perlman, H.H. (1952). *Casework: A Problem Solving Approach.* Chicago: University of Chicago Press.

Poertner, J. and A. Press (1990). "Who Best Represents the Interests of the Child in Court?" *Child Welfare.* LXIX:6. November-December. 194.

Priest, G.L. (1990). "The New Legal Structure of Risk Control." *Daedalus.* Fall. 119:4. 207.

Prout, C. and R.N. Ross (1989). *Care and Punishment: The Dilemmas of Prison Medicine.* Pittsburgh, PA: University of Pittsburgh Press.

Qualliotine, R. (1991). "The Legal Risks of Doing Peer Review Are Overblown." *Medical Economics.* January 21. 15.

Reamer, F.G. (1986). "The Use of Modern Technology in Social Work: Ethical Dilemmas." *Social Work.* 31:6. November-December. 469.

Reamer, F.G. (1987). "Ethics Committees in Social Work." *Social Work.* 32:3. May-June. 188.

Reamer, F. G. (1987). "Informed Consent in Social Work." *Social Work.* 32:5. September-October. 425.

Reamer, F.G. (1989). "Liability Issues in Social Work Supervision." *Social Work.* 34:5. September. 445.

Rohr, H. (1979). *Professional Accountability in Social Work Practice.* New York: Prodist.

Reid, W. (1978). *The Task-Centered System.* New York: Columbia University Press.

Rhodes, S.L. (1977). "Contract Negotiation in the Initial Stage of Casework Service." *Social Service Review.* Spring. 96.

Robinowitz, C. and M. Greenblatt (1980). "Continuing Education and Continuing Certification." *American Journal of Psychiatry.* 137:3. 291.

Sadoff, R. (1982). *Legal Issues in the Care of Psychiatric Patients.* New York: Springer.

Saltzman, A. (1986). "Reporting Child Abusers and Protecting Substance Abusers." *Social Work.* 31:6. November-December. 474.

Schroeder, L. (1982). *The Legal Environment of Social Work.* Englewood Cliffs, NJ: Prentice-Hall.

Schultz, L. G. (1989). "The Victimization of Social Workers." *Journal of Independent Social Work.* 3:3. 51.

Schultz, L.G. (1991). "Social Workers As Expert Witnesses: Guidelines for Courtroom Testimony." *Journal of Independent Social Work.* 5:2.

Schwartz, G. (1989). "Confidentiality Revisited." *Social Work.* 34:3. May. 223.

Seabury, B.A. (1987). "Contracting and Engagement in Direct Practice." *Enclyclopedia of Social Work, 18th Edition.* Silver Spring, MD: National Association of Social Workers. 339-345.

Seelig, J.M. (1989). "Tax Considerations in Legal Partnerships." *Journal of Independent Social Work.* 3:3. 103.

Seelig, J.M. (1988). "Drafting a Partnership Agreement." *Journal of Independent Social Work.* 2:3. 73.

Seelig, J.M. (1990). "Mandatory Continuing Education." *Journal of Independent Social Work.* 4:3. 75.

Segaloff, R. (1986). "The Care and Protection Battleground: When Lawyers and Social Workers Collide." *Boston Bar Journal.* March-April. 37.

Shamroy, J.A. (1987). "Interviewing the Sexually Abused Child with Anatomically Correct Dolls." *Social Work.* 32:2. March-April. 165.

Sharwell, G. (1982). "Avoiding Legal Liability in the Practice of School Social Work." *Journal of Social Work Education.* 5:3 October. 17.

Shuman, D.W. and M.S. Weiner (1990). "The Privilege Study: An

Empirical Examination of the Psychotherapist-Patient Privilege," in Wexler, D.B., ed., *Therapeutic Jurisprudence: The Law as a Therapeutic Agent.* Durham, NC: Carolina Academic Press.

Simmons, J. (1981). "Issues Raised by Tarasoff Case Causes Confusion to Psychiatrists, Courts." *Clinical Psychiatry News.* September 10.

Siporin, M. (1982). "Moral Philosophy in Social Work Today." *Social Service Review.* 56(4). May.

Skidmore, S.L. (1990). "Suggested Standards for Child Abuse Evaluations." *Psychotherapy in Private Practice.* 8:2. 25.

Sloane, H. (1967). "Relationship of Law and Social Work." *Social Work.* 12:1. 86.

Slovenko, R. (1968). *Psychotherapy, Confidentiality and Privileged Communication.* Springfield, IL: Charles C Thomas Co.

Spakes, P. (1987). "Social Workers and the Courts." *Journal of Social Work Education.* 14:2. 29.

Spaulding, E.C. (1989). *Statistics on Social Work Education in the United States: 1988.* Washington, DC: Council on Social Work Education.

Sporakowski, M. (1982). "The Regulation of Marital and Family Therapy." L. L'Abate, ed., *Values, Ethics, Legalities, and the Family Therapist.* Rockville, MD: Aspen Publications.

Stehno, S. M. (1987). "Juvenile Courts, Probation and Parole." *Encyclopedia of Social Work, 18th Edition.* Silver Spring, MD: National Association of Social Workers. 2-6.

Sundel, M. and S. Sundel (1985). *Behavioral Modification in the Human Services, 2nd Edition.* Englewood Cliffs, NJ: Prentice-Hall.

Taft, J.J. (1936). *Functional Approaches in Social Case Work.* Philadelphia: University of Pennsylvania.

Tarasoff v. Regents of the University of California (1976). *California Law Reporter.* 14, 551, p. 2d, 334.

Thyer, B.A. and M.A. Biggerstaff (1989). *Professional Social Work, Credentialing, and Legal Regulation.* Springfield, IL: Charles C Thomas.

Valentine, P.W. (1990). "College Park Psychiatrist, 2 Aides Sentenced in Prescription Case." *The Washington Post.* Jan 21.

Van Hoose, W.H. and J.A. Kottler (1985). *Ethical and Legal Issues in Counseling and Psychotherapy.* San Francisco, CA: Jossey-Bass.

Wald, M.S. and M. Woolverton (1990). "Risk Assessment: The Emperor's New Clothes?" *Child Welfare.* LXIX:6. November-December.

Watkins, S.A. and J.C. Watkins (1983). "Malpractice in Clinical Social Work: A Perspective on Civil Liability in the 1980s." *Behavioral Sciences and the Law.* 1:1. 55. 90.

Watkins, S.A. and J.C. Watkins (1989). "Negligent Endangerment: Malpractice in a Clinical Context." *Journal of Independent Social Work.* 3:3. 35.

Watkins, S.A. (1989). "Confidentiality and Privileged Communications: Legal Dilemma for Family Therapists." *Social Work.* 34:2 March. 133.

Weimer, I. and A. Heirs (1987). *Handbook of Forensic Psychology.* Somerset, NJ: Wiley and Sons.

Wexler, D.B. (1990). *Therapeutic Jurisprudence: The Law as a Therapeutic Agent.* Durham, NC: Carolina Academic Press.

Whiting, L. (1991). "State Comparisons of Laws Regulating Social Work." (Unpublished photocopy.) Silver Spring, MD: National Association of Social Workers.

Wilcoxon, S.A. (1988). "Legal and Ethical Issues in Consultation." *Journal of Independent Social Work.* 3:2. 47.

Wodarski, J.S., M. Saffir, and M. Frazer (1982). "Using Research to Evaluate the Effectiveness of Task Centered Casework." *Journal of Applied Social Sciences.* 7:1. 70.

Yates, A. (1987). "Should Young Children Testify in Cases of Sexual Abuse?" *American Journal of Psychiatry.* 144:4.1. 1476-80.

Zastrow, C. (1991). "Safeguarding Rights in NASW Processes for Adjudication of Grievances." *Journal of Independent Social Work.* 5:2.

Index

Predicting client behavior, 27-28,36, 40,49
Premature termination, 38-39,57,59, 86
Prescribing medications, 37,38
Presentation of testimony, 10,19
Preventive practice against malpractice, 30-31
Private practice, 77,80
Probation officers, 3,8
Professional associations, 52,72,74, 76,88,89,103
Professional certification, 71
Professional conferences emphasis on law, 6
Professional ethics, 19
Professional sanctions, 9
Professional standards, 9,14,25,30, 72,76
Proponent lawyer, 20
Prosecuting attorney, 51
Psychiatry profession, 75
Psychology profession, 75,79
Psychosocial orientation and contracting, 56-57
Public regulation of social workers, 4
Punishment for substandard performance (*See* sanctions)

Qualifications for licensure, 74,75
Qualifying the expert, 20
Quality controls, 72

Rape, 13,33
Reagan Administration, 80
Reciprocity of licenses, 74,82
Redirect examination, 20
Reexamination for licenses, 83-84
Referral to other professionals, 37-38,52
Registration as a credential, 73-74
Rehearsing as expert witness, 19
Relatives' responsibility, 1
Release of information, 34

Reporting client behavior (*See* confidentiality)
Resistance in therapy, 57
Respondeat Superior doctrine, 103
Retaining the lawyer, 111-112
Risks of liability, 9,60
Risks of treatment, 32,36,40

Sanctions, 11,38,43,72-73,87,96
steps to minimize, 97
types of, 89-90
Sanity determination, 13
Second opinions, 39
Sequester, 20
Sexual impropriety, 31,33,93
Short-term therapy, 57
Social agencies, 77
Social control function, 50
Specialist versus generalist legal counsel, 110
Spouse abuse, 8
Standard of care, 28,29,32-41
Subpoena, 18,68
Subpoena duces tecum, 105
Substandard professional practice, 28,29,30
Suicide, 26,29,31,36-37
Sunset legislation, 79
Supervisor, 4,48,77,78,80
Supervisor liability, 48,51,103-104
Surrebuttal, 20
Swearing in to testify, 20

Task-centered social work, 57
Tarasoff case, 40-41,46-48,102
Terminating treatment, 38-39,66
Testimony, providing expert witness, 13-24,109
procedures in presenting, 20-22
Therapy outcomes, 27
Third party, 72,73,75,76,77,78,79, 82,83,86,87,88,89
influences in contracting, 58-59
review procedures, 90-91
Transference in treatment, 39,57